Barry Pilton was born in 1946 in Croydon, and educated at Dulwich College and King's College, London. In 1967–8 he lived in Paris and taught English. In 1969 he worked in Fleet Street as a journalist for the *Sunday Post*. Before eventually becoming a freelance writer in 1976 he trained unsuccessfully as a surveyor, a fork-lift truck driver, a furniture removal man, a cooking-oil operative, and a dishwasher; on days off he travelled extensively in Europe, the Middle East, North Africa and the U.S.A. Since 1984 he has lived in mid-Wales.

TV work includes sit-coms *Shelley* and *It Takes A Worried Man*, comedy show *Not The Nine O'Clock News*, and the play *Slimming Down*. Extensive radio work ranges from Radio 3 talks to documentary series, sketch shows and situation comedy. These include *The 27 Year Itch*, *Weekending*, *The Jason Explanation*, *Miles of London*, and *Degrees of Humour*, a history of the Cambridge Footlights. He also broadcasts occasionally, was a contributor to the live chat show *Extra Dry Sherrin*, and has written for *Punch*.

One Man and His Bog started life as a Radio 4 series of talks.

One Man and His Bog

Barry Pilton

CORGI BOOKS

ONE MAN AND HIS BOG

A CORGI BOOK 0 552 12796 5

First publication in Great Britain

PRINTING HISTORY
Corgi edition published 1986

This book is set in 10/11 pt Plantin

Corgi Books are published by Transworld Publishers Ltd.,
61–63 Uxbridge Road, Ealing, London W5 5SA, in Australia
by Transworld Publishers (Aust.) Pty. Ltd., 26 Harley
Crescent, Condell Park, NSW 2200, and in New Zealand by
Transworld Publishers (N.Z.) Ltd., Cnr. Moselle and
Waipareira Avenues, Henderson, Auckland.

Made and printed in Great Britain by
Hunt Barnard Printing Ltd., Aylesbury, Bucks.

Contents

Author's Note

If this book should in some small way encourage people to take up walking themselves, then the author suggests that they read the book again more carefully.

Cartographer's note

These maps are not to scale. Nor are they an accurate representation of any of the places shown thereon. Nor do they in any way imply, or suggest, the existence, or otherwise, of any such places, here or elsewhere. Any similarity with any features is purely coincidental or malicious. These maps are particularly not recommended for use in mist.

MAP 1

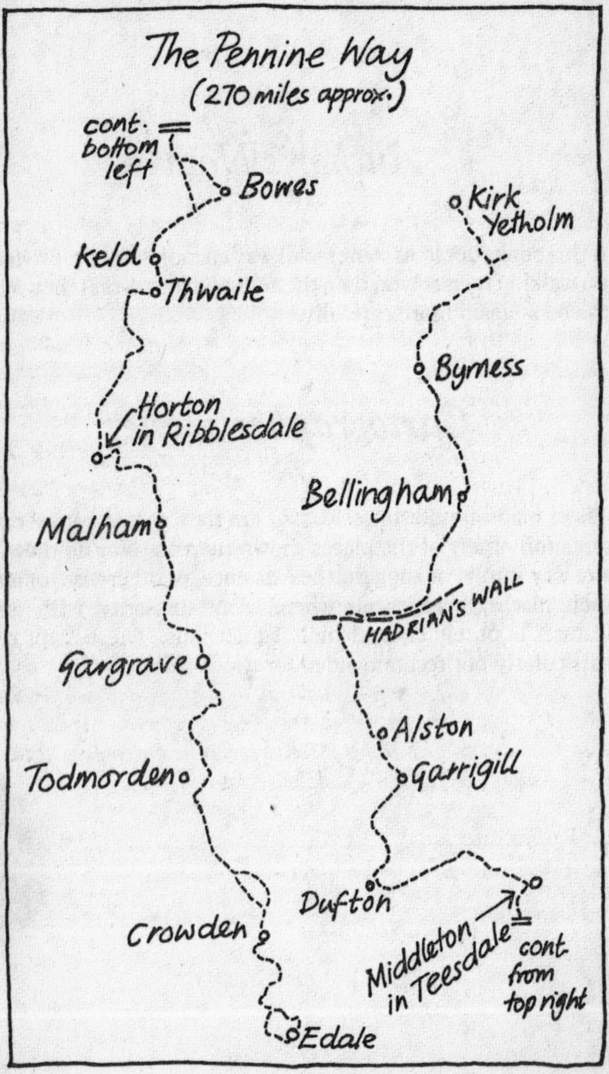

The Pennine Way
(270 miles approx.)

cont. bottom left

Bowes

Kirk Yetholm

Keld
Thwaite

Byrness

Horton in Ribblesdale

Bellingham

Malham

HADRIAN'S WALL

Gargrave

Alston
Garrigill

Todmorden

Dufton

Crowden

Middleton in Teesdale
cont. from top right

Edale

Foreword

Anyone who has ever walked the Pennine Way will relish every mile of this book, anyone who has never walked it cannot fail but to enjoy this literary journey for he will travel with Barry Pilton through the peat bogs and over the limestone pavements of the Pennines in the company, not of a great, but of an honest explorer – the sort of Captain Oates who would have stayed in the tent and said 'You bugger off out Scott – it was your idea in the first place.'

I walked the Pennine Way a couple of years ago and know exactly where the pub is near Thornton in Craven with the Fascist landlord that won't allow hikers in his 'best room' and I too encountered the grim wastes of Sleightholme Moor, only I was the wally who went across the moor and got so lost that I became the only human example of Brownian motion.

This book made me relive all those long miles and laugh at them all over again, but if I ever see a large shambling figure lurching towards me through the mist, mushrooms growing from his rucksack and albatross about his neck, I shall avoid him like the bogs of Black Hill for 'twill be none other than B. Pilton Esq., the *Marie Celeste* of Kinder Scout.

Mike Harding
President of the Ramblers' Association

1 FOREWALK

It was some time last year when I first realised that I no longer had an uninterrupted view of my feet. Several medical textbooks diagnosed the problem as middle age, a condition with no known cure. Indeed, this most contagious of diseases can be held in check by only one, highly unpleasant, course of treatment – what leading physicians privately describe as 'exercise'. So I decided to take a walk.

The Pennine Way is Britain's longest walk, running from the Peak District to the Cheviots, a distance of between 250 and 300 miles, depending on how often you get lost and how much you like to exaggerate. It is called a high-level walk (which means one goes from A to B via mountain-tops C to Z) and it has been claimed – probably under the influence of oxygen starvation – that all its ascents added together would total over 32,000 feet, which is Everest plus the uneroded bit of Snowdon. The reason, however, that people climb Everest is 'because it is there' – a major challenge of the Pennine Way is that frequently it isn't there, since an unpleasant feature of watersheds does tend to be water, usually in the form of man-eating bogs which have swallowed the path as an hors d'oeuvre. And if the bogs don't get you, the mist will.

I do not have the best walking credentials – I usually walk by car – so I approached the three week trek with a commendable degree of caution; indeed, I filled my borrowed rucksack with so many contingency planning items that I was unable to lift it. Maps, bandages, whistle; fluorescent red anorak so the rescue helicopter could spot me easily; and enough Kendal mint-cake to make a profit-

7

able living as one of their salesmen. I was also weighed down with advice, of which the best, in retrospect, was not to go at all.

But go I did, one Saturday afternoon in June from St Pancras Railway Station – and quickly found even suburbia is not without its challenge. Alone in front of my bedroom mirror, smugly preening myself in all the macho gear of A Walker, I had rather fancied my public image would be akin to Monarch of the Glen. Out on the streets I soon learnt that boots and a bulging rucksack are, to the urban eye, merely a sure sign that one has no home to go to and has arrived, socially, at the stage immediately prior to becoming a meths drinker. Even on the train, few passengers seemed to appreciate I was travelling on a rare Marco Polo Away Day ticket.

It was a warm summery evening when the local whistle-stop train arrived at the Derbyshire village of Edale, home of the Pennine Way starting blocks. The village nestled in all the comforting domestic rurality of cows and sheep and fields and things. Down the valley, the setting sun was posing for a picture postcard, and everywhere Nature was making it clear that at least She loved a walker.

I made my way to the Youth Hostel, a mile distant. As I remembered them, Youth Hostels used to be reassuring sanctuaries, full of spotty cyclists, butterfly-lovers and believers in the values that made Sparta great, such as outside toilets. Hostels were refuges, communities where lovers of the simple life in shorts would gather to discuss the latest in wild flowers, and sing healthy walking songs. The first song that I heard on approaching Edale Youth Hostel was a rather rude punk number, which the disco loudspeakers pounded through several floors, causing the giant Coca-Cola machines to vibrate gently. Then, as I unlaced my Sherpa Tensing boots, a school party of teenage boys rampaged past in pursuit of a school party of teenage girls, whom they apparently wished to engage in field studies. And when I went to the rest-room, I found it being used to rehearse the next round of inner-city riots.

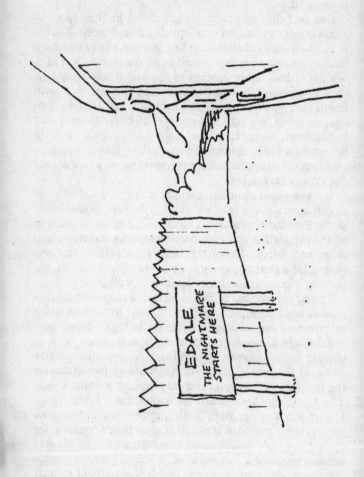

EDALE
THE NIGHTMARE STARTS HERE

So, feeling something of a freak in my red bobbly hat, I settled down outside on the grass, tore the cellophane off my new compass and opened the instruction manual on how to use it for map-reading. An hour's close study made it clear to me that each of the surrounding hills had been placed in the wrong position, presumably by a lax National Parks Authority. I turned to the page which explained how to find North just by pointing the hands of a watch at the sun. (The technique with a digital watch was unclear.) Unfortunately, by the time I had fully mastered the theory, the sun had gone down, sinking gloriously in the East.

I decided to concentrate instead on my sleep. All the D.I.Y. explorer's books are very keen on sleep, and recommend at least a night's worth every twenty-four hours. Unhappily, I was in a dormitory of hyper-active primary schoolchildren, and this viewpoint put me in a minority of one. Apparently, none of the children had ever been in any wide open spaces larger than a cage before. First, we had the running about, then the rude noises, then the stealing of blankets, then the rustling of crisp packets, and finally the tying of a dozen empty Coca-Cola cans to a pyjama cord, which was then lowered from the window to scare witless their little mates in the dormitory below. Nowhere do the great Victorian explorers like Burton or Livingstone mention such problems. In all, I spent an exhausting, almost sleepless, night, in which fevered visions of Hieronymus Bosch landscapes played a major part, and gradually my mental preparedness evaporated. Even the passing of time itself had difficulty that night, and around 4 a.m. my watch – presumably worried by the prospect of learning new tricks – came to a full stop, and was quite immune to any winding. A vigorous, no-nonsense shake caused both hands to fall off, severely reducing my chances of making it to the North Pole, and I began to feel a very ill-starred voyager. Over the coming weeks, though, I was to feel alone in space as well as time.

2 A FAREWELL TO LEGS

Next morning, all my planning was thwarted because the sun failed to rise East, West or anywhere.

Rather alarmed by the driving rain and off-black skies, I consulted two books from amongst the small library I was carrying. Describing the opening section of the route, the first said that, in view of the dangers of the 2,000 ft Kinder Scout plateau in mist and rain, 'a postponement was preferable to a post mortem'. The second said that as the area had 65 inches of rain a year, it could pour non-stop for weeks on end.

Now very alarmed, I sought a walking companion at breakfast. 'I'm setting off to walk the Pennine Way,' I said with casual modesty to a couple of strapping young six-footers, over our energy-rich cornflakes.

'Oh aye,' they said. 'We set off yesterday.' And they launched upon an epic tale of human endurance, describing how they had wandered helplessly lost for over fourteen hours, in conditions of brilliant sunshine – the reason being, I learnt, that Kinder Scout is Britain's contribution to The International Year of The Swamp.

Alone, and extremely alarmed, I loaded up and set off in a steady downpour towards the great grey yonder. I went into the nearby National Parks Centre to check the local forecast and learnt that not only was I now enjoying the *good* part of the day, but also that walkers to Crowden, that night's destination, were advised to forewarn the Mountain Rescue Team. The card that I had to fill in came complete with space for next of kin. The last of my morale ebbed away through my tasteful Norwegian woolly socks when I

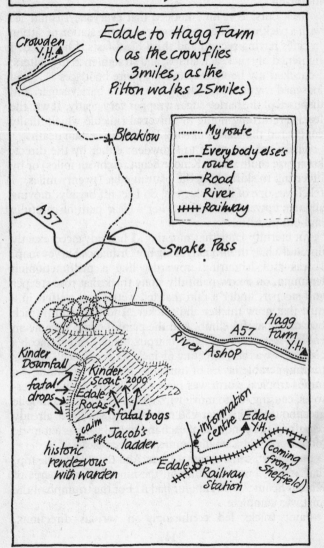

MAP 2: (DAY 1)

Edale to Hagg Farm
(as the crow flies
3 miles, as the
Pilton walks 25 miles)

Crowden Y.H.

Bleaklow

A 57

Snake Pass

Hagg Farm Y.H.

River Ashop

A 57

Kinder Downfall

fatal drops

Kinder Scout 2000

Edale Rocks

fatal bogs

cairn

Jacob's ladder

historic rendezvous with warden

information centre

Edale Y.H.

Edale

Edale Railway Station

(coming from Sheffield)

My route
Everybody else's route
Road
River
Railway

found that the Estimated Time of Arrival for serious walkers would seem to involve me in the hire of a motor-bike.

Back outside again I noticed that everyone I could see with a pack was either walking towards the station or sitting in cafés having second and third breakfasts. I hesitated. I tightened my rucksack straps, and straightened my gaiters; I checked my bootlaces, and my spare bootlaces . . . and loosened my rucksack straps, and had a barley sugar, and disposed of the barley sugar wrapper very neatly. It was the fear of returning home to universal ridicule which finally conquered the fear of moving forward to certain death.

There are two ways to Crowden: either by the direct, kamikaze route across Kinder Scout (eighteen miles) or by diverting to skirt along the plateau edge (twenty miles). I felt I was one of life's skirters. So I set off briskly, moving slightly upwards, and following a clear path of carefully laid-out puddles.

An eternity later that morning, I had advanced exactly one and a half thumbnails along my Ordnance Survey map. I was still labouring upwards, like a malfunctioning lemming, on a now painfully stony track that rose steeper and steeper, under a rain that fell wetter and wetter, in a mist that grew thicker and thicker. And the painful track became a painful climb, and the painful climb became an endless series of walkers' hairpin bends, called Jacob's Ladder. I was also sweating 65 inches a year since – thanks to innumerable layers of luminous protective clothing – a minor tropical storm was raging inside my Alpine under-wear, causing me to move with all the panache of a mobile greenhouse. With over 250 miles still to go, I was already regarding the conquest of each individual yard as a tour de force worthy of a small commemorative plaque.

Suddenly I came across a cairn. And that meant the top, that at last I was standing on the nine thousand acres of Kinder Scout. Or so rumour had it. For the triumph of the mist was complete.

Faint tracks led confusingly in various directions,

14

vanishing into the half-light and the soggy peat; it reminded me of the film setting for the swamp in *The Hound Of The Baskervilles*, where actors are lost at the rate of one per day. Several times I made exploratory moves forward; each time, the cairn, lighthouse of my life, would quickly fade from view, and I made panic-stricken moves backward. In the end, I devoted all my energies to just leaning against the cairn.

It was not yet noon on Day One, and already I was at a complete loss. Panic was gripping those parts of the body that other fears cannot reach. Tomorrow's cornflakes at Edale Youth Hostel would see my turn to be a cautionary tale.

Suddenly, an old man emerged from the mist. 'Not too much sun today,' he said as he went to pass by. Before my eyes flashed a vision of Hardy novels, where all the climactic events take place at cross-roads on lonely moors, and – desperate to detain him – I heard myself actually saying, 'Are you from these parts, sir?' He paused. 'I'm the Ranger,' he said.

I would like to nominate this man for a knighthood.

In his sixties, dressed in the walking style of the Thirties, his was a deeply reassuring presence. He not only directed me to the right set of bootmarks, and offered me a brand of glucose sweets I had not yet tried, but he also went out of his way for me. It was with great self-restraint that I refrained from asking if he fancied a walk to Scotland. Keen to conceal my previous panic, I strove to impress him with the sturdy professionalism of my walking. Unfortunately, this proved difficult to do from behind; he strode effortlessly on, up hillock and down ditch, with an all-consuming rhythmic gait, like a camel in knickerbockers. Unerringly, he guided me to the crucial landmark of Edale Rocks, a massive outcrop which that day dominated the landscape for inches around.

Here he stopped. We chatted. Personally, I favoured a good lie-down and a nap, but I suspected this was not a Ranger custom. He provided me with a few useful pointers

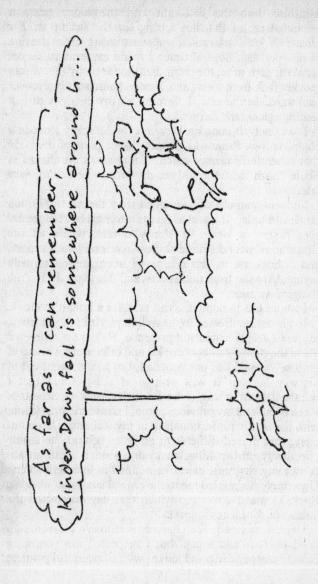

As far as I can remember, Kinder Downfall is somewhere around h....

– such as the general direction of the sheer cliff edge nearby – and then he picked up his pack. I tried to think of conversational topics with a lifespan of several years, but even my larynx felt waterlogged. Before leaving, he told me, by way of interesting social chit-chat, that a recent survey had shown 75 per cent of all walkers give up the Pennine Way – halfway through the first day, when the hypothetical path crosses a very real bus route. And he added, with the clear implication that I was so far only on the kiddies' section, that the high terrain *beyond* the A59, aptly called Bleaklow, 'could be tricky in mist'. One of my books put it differently. It said people had died up there. And then he was gone.

Almost immediately I realised I was now lost both in front *and* behind! For a map to be of help in such weather, the scale needs to be approximately one mile to the mile. All I knew was that somewhere ahead of me lay Kinder Downfall – a dramatic cascade off the plateau, one of the Seven Wonders of the Walk . . . somewhere!

If mist were a government responsibility, the State would be sued for criminal sensory deprivation. I stumbled on; pea-soup around me, peat-soup below me, rain percolating throughout me; keeping the plateau edge to the left, the Battle of the Somme area to the right; and, all in all, deciding I had been seriously misled about the nature of country walks.

After a second eternity in one day, I finally found the waterfall – but I never did see it. To my astonishment, what I did come across, hidden in rock crevices and under boulders, were little knots of bedraggled ramblers, listening to the sound of the view. This greatly encouraged me, it made my venture seem part of a *wider* human plan of total madness; I was reluctant to move on again because the possibility of dying from exposure *in a group* seemed a great improvement to my circumstances. But I was also reluctant to stand still, knowing that hypothermia finds it more difficult to hit a moving target.

I tried to shelter, and discovered that not only·was the

rain horizontal but the wind was circular – each an aspect of weather that Mr Michael Fish has never seen fit to make public; I tried to change pullovers 26 and 27 at speed, and found it was a procedure normally restricted to circus acts; I tried to eat my packed lunch, and watched my fingers go the colour and texture of deep-frozen celery.

I felt it was essential to move on, but it was also essential to find someone else moving on in my direction . . . whichever direction that was in. I did not wish to appear helpless – I even prepared excuses about having broken my compass in the Himalayas – but I did want to seem a serious candidate for the position of walker's companion. It seemed best to approach fellow walkers casually yet vir-ilely, but the only words that kept coming to mind were, 'I want my Mummy!' So instead I pottered to and fro silently in the gloom, trying to look the type of rambler you would want to take home to muffins and tea.

My luck was in – again. This time I managed to team up with a life-long walker, a local man, middle-aged yet so expert in his knowledge of the moors that he needed neither map nor encumbering rucksack. Indeed, he gave the firm impression that he relied on an innate sense of magnetic north. So with great élan, we descended from the plateau, and then fairly charged up and down the hills, for hour after hour . . . after hour. And hill after hill . . . after hill. In such weather all hills can look very much the same. It was only after considerable debate, and less élan, we finally agreed they were the same.

By then we were sufficiently deep in bracken to qualify for a camouflage certificate from the marines; rainwater had penetrated so comprehensively that, when I moved, even my armpits squelched; and we were clinging to the sort of slope normally photographed with goats on. Worse, my physical condition was fast deteriorating – even allowing for the importance of liquid to the human body, I thought that for my particular body to be 100 per cent water seemed excessive, if indeed not of interest to medical science. I was, I feared, about to become a puddle.

18

It was in these less-than-successful circumstances that my companion grudgingly admitted to 'a minor miscalculation'. He also admitted he was 'out of practice', and announced this to be his first proper outing for over two years. He then told me the story of his major coronary failure.

I felt I had crossed that narrow line between tragedy and farce. Some hours earlier, I had come to accept that I might make the next day's headlines in my capacity as a corpse; what I had not realised was that before meeting my Maker, I might be required to bury someone else. This would test even *my* first-aid supplies. The position was now serious. I would have uttered a few well-chosen words of hikerly abuse, but feared lest I upset his convalescent blood pressure; blue – though a favourite colour of mine – is not an ideal shade for a face.

Yoked together by joint incompetence, we opted for a gentler pace, one more suited to the slow, careful step of The Funeral March. We also decided to follow the stream we were standing in, on the dubious grounds that it alone appeared to know where it was going. I was now so demoralised that it would have been no surprise to find it developed into the Clyde, or just possibly the Ganges. Nor would I have cared much.

To cut a very long walk short, I did manage the twenty miles that day . . . of which some dozen were in concentric and very bad-tempered circles with a man who had clearly spent so much of his life walking because he had all the navigational sense of a headless chicken. Finally, after following the river for long hours of descent and dissent, a watery sun came out. It was in the wrong position again. Then the A59 appeared, also in the wrong position. Then my companion's wife appeared, with a car, and in he got, and off they drove, waving.

I followed the trunk road for miles, trying to get it to fit my map. It was not a success. Nothing was a success. My first day of the great adventure ended with me wetter than if I had fallen the length of Kinder Downfall, stiffer than a

bad case of *rigor mortis* and spending the night, as the solitary and less-than-happy occupant, at Hagg Farm Youth Hostel, described in the handbook as three miles from Edale. And further from Crowden than when I had started.*

*Before finally keeling over, I did remember to ring the Mountain Rescue Team and tell them I was safe. For professional reasons, I omitted to say exactly where I was.

3 MUCK AND BILLETS

Day Two. I had aged considerably overnight. Several key limbs seemed to be loose, and my other bits no longer responded to simple commands like Stand Up; Sit Down; Turn Around; Go Home. I also had a problem with my rucksack – or my equipment, as we walkers call it. It was wet, it was very mucky, and it was quietly steaming. Conditions inside made it more suitable for use as a gardener's growbag. Should the world be inadvertently destroyed during my walk, I was now carrying enough basic ingredients of primeval gunge to get the whole messy business of Creation off the ground again. The Peak District is strong on primeval gunge. Although the Tourist Board tends to underplay this, it is provided to a depth slightly greater than the average rambler's height; probably the first prehistoric female mud-wrestlers came from this area.

My spirit was equally dampened as the first task of the day was to re-spool the mis-spent miles of the previous day, a gross misuse of my scarce natural resources. Although the initial direction was clear – the A59 is one of the country's better-marked tracks – I failed to warm (metaphorically, that is) to the joys of the open trunk road, and a few sole-destroying miles of *terra tarmaca* almost produced a longing for some homely quicksands. Even the arrival of perfect visibility for the first time in twenty-four hours seemed a shade mocking as I had no intention of taking the bends at more than 40 m.p.h. Eventually, I reached the torrent of yesterday, where, with much despair, I realised that I had to turn due South, a perverse way of approaching Scotland. The map was unequivocal: I had to follow the

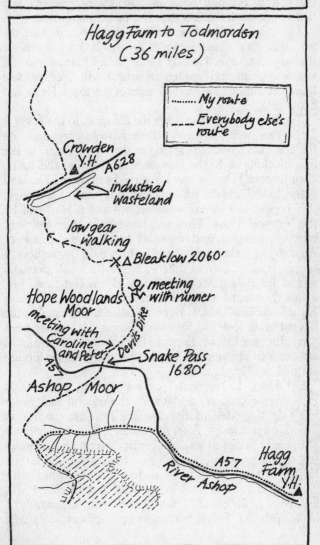

MAP 3: SECT. A

Hagg Farm to Todmorden
(36 miles)

········· My route
- - - - Everybody else's
route

Crowden
Y.H.   A628
→ industrial
wasteland

low gear
walking
×△ Bleaklow 2060'

meeting
with runner

Hope Woodlands
Moor

meeting with
Caroline
and Peter

Devil's Dike

Snake Pass
1680'

A57

Ashop Moor

River Ashop   A57   Hagg
Farm
Y.H.

river into the hills until it vanished up its own source. That took until late lunchtime. It was little satisfaction to know that halfway through the second day I was back where I was halfway through the first day. But rather more tired.

The great disadvantage of mist is that one cannot see the way. The great disadvantage of no mist is that one can see the way. And ahead, as far as the naked binocular could see, was grim and sodden moorland. All the available literature indicated at least 40 miles of goo to go. Heart and boots sank.

The first target was to cover the 2½ miles to the 1,680 ft Snake Pass, well-known star of severe weather reports. (As the first cuckoo heralds spring to the nature-lover, so the first blocking of Snake Pass heralds winter to the Radio Four listener.) On the way I observed a mystery. The land is featureless, almost post-nuclear in lay-out; it is dreary, it is boggy, it is devoid of interest – and it is owned by the National Trust. They are, however, a huge and very busy organisation, and obviously bought it sight unseen. Anyone can make a mistake. As a fully paid-up member, I simply made a mental note to request a small personal refund for Ashop Moor, and carried on. But then, just across the road, I found the same con-man had sold them Hope Woodlands Moor. Hope Woodlands Moor makes the blasted heath look like Sherwood Forest. If there are trees there, they are hiding. Even the fence posts were stunted. I am not a trouble-maker, but I think the membership are entitled to an explanation.

But where the National Trust were remiss, the National Park were excessively zealous. At the edge of each moor was a list of regulations that made the Ten Commandments look like a postscript. After forbidding me to do all manner of unlikely things to animals, birds, direction posts, milestones, fences, gates, plants, roots, trees and game, it then further advised me against undesirable behaviour with guns, cars, rubbish and sheep. And just in case I still wanted to go for a walk, I was warned not to 'unlawfully or maliciously cut, break, bark, root up or otherwise destroy or damage any tree, sapling, shrub or undergrowth, thereby doing damage to the amount of 5p at least.' The penalty was three months (no wonder our jails are so full – ramblers are the new criminal class) or a £5 fine. It would be more effective to give a £5 reward to anyone actually finding a tree.

The High Peaks may be the 'Lungs of the Midlands', but they are lungs of the diseased, blackened and shrivelled variety that one usually finds in terminally-ill cigarette smokers. Here nature is not so much red in tooth and claw as black in gums and bowels. Such were the heretical thoughts that oozed to mind as I scrabbled up Devil's Dike on 2,060 ft Bleaklow ('low' meaning high, and 'bleak' being a similar understatement.)

Devil's Dike is a grough. A grough is an evil-smelling, sheer-sided, cavernous, treacly black ditch set in a morass of crumbling peat, and the Pennine Way has several million of them. Movement, difficult in any direction, is like stumbling around inside a giant's crotch.

Caroline said it all made for a very pleasant change. As did boy-friend Peter. Both students, I had made contact with them – as a barnacle to a rock – because they seemed to know their groughs. But we had a cultural barrier: they were actually *enjoying* themselves – an incomprehensible state of mind I was to encounter increasingly over the next few weeks. Rather like those mystifying people whose idea of sexual pleasure is to be roundly, soundly whipped, so too there is a mutant strain of walker whose idea of physical pleasure is to stride through peat bogs – an activity that Jesus himself rejected in favour of the much-easier walking on water. The point of a walk, for straightforward blokes like me and Wordsworth, is the aesthetics of beauty; for some hikers, a good view seems merely an optional extra.

We had been slithering together for over an hour when an even more alien being came into sight. A runner. Plimsolls, shorts, T shirt and rucksack, but no sign that he had escaped from anywhere. We all paused, sinking slowly, to exchange information; his information was that he had

earlier been trapped waist-deep for three hours on Black Hill. Black Hill was the next day's hill – it is obligatory on the Pennine Way that any walker you meet has always just come from somewhere even more appalling and impassable than where you are now. He had finally been dragged out, he added, by a chance passer-by. And then he bounded off again, showing an unclean pair of heels, and confirming my belief that jogging should fall under Section 3 of the Mental Health Act.

After conquering the squalid, ambiguous blob of a summit, walking underknee greatly improved, but it was still early evening before we had our first view of Crowden, far below in Longdendale valley. It was agreed that Caroline and Peter go on ahead, because although I was trying hard to imitate their gazelle-like pace, the result was felt to be more the speed of a dead gazelle. The descent was long and steep. When I arrived they had already pitched their tent, had a shower, cooked a three course meal, washed up, read two books, sung a camping song, and gone to bed.

I hobbled on to the very basic hostel. What I could see of Crowden by twilight was equally basic and not encouraging. There were no houses, just the desolate bric à brac of industrial rape – electricity pylons, railway tracks, waterworks, telegraph poles. I went to bed. Lying, dying, on my bunk, I felt on balance it had probably not been worth the two day walk.

I slept for just one painful hour that night. If the hostel had had a sprinkler system it would have been set off by the burning heat of my feet. When Greeks have feet like mine, they claim bastinado, and half the armed forces are charged with torture. In Britain, no one has yet successfully prosecuted a moor.

At breakfast I met a Glaswegian father and son going South, who assured me the Scottish end of the walk was even more appalling and impassable, and spoke patriotically of flash floods rising to 10 ft within seconds. That was the extent of the social life at Crowden. I met no one else, despite hanging around waiting for adoption until nearly

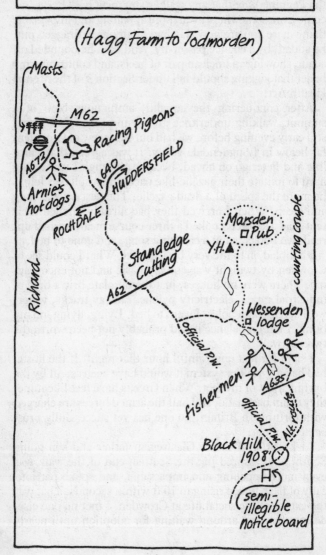

MAP 3: SECT. B

(Hagg Farm to Todmorden)

Masts

M62

Racing Pigeons

A672

Arnie's hot dogs

A640

HUDDERSFIELD

ROCHDALE

Richard

Stanedge Cutting

A62

Marsden Pub

Y.H.

Wessenden lodge

courting couple

official P.W.

fishermen

A635

official P.W.

Alt. route

Black Hill 1908

semi-illegible notice board

mid-morning. I greatly feared the jogger's fate. No one, from Defoe onwards, had had a good word to say about the coming miles.

The windswept summit of 1,908 ft Black Hill is the start of Yorkshire. If one is to give up anywhere, it is here. It is the landscape of a nightmare moon – endless, grassless black dunes that plunge on all sides into bottomless black pools of evil liquid mud. If ever a path could be sued under The Trades Descriptions Act, it is this one. I had only to *think* of moving and the ground squelched, like a diner smacking his lips. Retreat was as implausible as advance, for every step so far had been a mistake. Even the absence of the mist was a mixed blessing as it had been removed by a hurricane. The visibility was good, but the paralysis total. The only things to move were two jam sandwiches and an orange which the wind transferred to Lancashire at twice the speed of sound. Just standing still itself was a challenge, for here he who hesitated was blown away as well as lost. My waterproofs, a failure against water, responded to wind by converting into a spinnaker. I soon discovered the only way to remain upright was by tying a reef knot in each arm.

I squatted down, like a small bell-tent, to think; to panic; and to pray. I had read somewhere that, as a result of road schemes and tunnel schemes and reservoir schemes, an irreversible drying-out process was now underway throughout the Peak District, and would eventually expose the gritstone bedrock of the entire National Park. I wondered if I had time to wait. My only other hope was the two old ladies in a Morris Minor whom I had seen on Monday. They had stopped beside the road, produced a spade, shook open a black plastic binliner and carefully filled it with large dollops of peat. I reckoned that if their needs for fuel become really severe there was just an outside chance they might accidentally dig their way through to me. Such are the fantasies of desperation.

After some time studying this desolate landscape I spotted a distant and almost inaccessibly water-bound noticeboard. At great personal risk I accessed to it; it said

'Dogs to be Kept on a Lead.' Surrealism is not a quality I had previously associated with town clerks. The only other high-point of that God-forsaken day was the relief of my rucksack hitting the ground; unfortunately it was the result of the strap breaking.

Clearly, I did get through; equally clearly, I would not like the job of guide.

At several points on the Pennine Way there is a choice of itinerary, called an Official Alternative, whose use does not qualify one for a white feather. This is usually like offering a condemned man a choice of poisons: a quick bog or a slow bog. But after Black Hill, there is the Wessenden Alternative. This offers a choice of marsh and slime or cakes and tea. No contest.

As I creaked my way down a stony track off the moors, I saw the first signs of civilisation for days – a parked car with steamed-up windows and an excess number of plaited legs on the back seat. A few hundred yards more in the teeming rain, and I passed two fishermen sitting by a small reservoir, although whether they were alive or dead I could not tell. And then I came to the flesh-pot Wessenden House, one of the very rare cafés en route. Unfortunately, it had gone out of business.

I decided to call it a day and detour a further two miles down the track to the Youth Hostel at Marsden. I felt ready for giant Coca-Cola machines and the soft life. Unfortunately, the hostel was closed for repairs.

Air travel is surprisingly similar to high-level walking in its effects. (Though you do get less jet-lag on most walks.) A plane dumps you without cultural preamble in a foreign land. And so too does walking alone over the hills keep you unaware of the changes below. Suddenly, I was in the North.

As I stumbled down to Marsden, after three days in the wilderness, I found myself in the land of mills and high chimneys. Three days of silence, and now the language was full of apostrophes. I had tangible evidence of my progress.

The sun was out, the cobbles were drying, the air smelt post-industrial. And I felt happy. As I looked down the steep streets to the small town, bells echoed up to greet me. It was another sign of civilisation, they were ice-cream bells. Unfortunately, I failed to attain the 2 m.p.h. needed to reach the van in time.

I stayed the night in a pub opposite the gasometer. I had a great time. It was full of warm-hearted, lively people who, with comforting normality, drank toasts to the proposition that all walkers were mad. The saloon bar radiated the sort of glow usually only seen in beer commercials. I sat back in an easy chair, jokes and drink spilling around me, and watched the darts thud in. Several buxom wenches asked me to play pool, but naturally, because of my condition, I had to refuse.

I did pop outside once for a breath of fish and chips, and found a member of the Holme Valley Moorland Rescue team loitering nearby. Clearly, he had been advised of my presence in town and, hearing of my problems with navigation, had decided to see I made it to the chippie safely. As I tottered down the street, I could not help noticing that, like me, the town was on its uppers. The buildings all showed tell-tale signs that the Industrial Black Death of the 80s had passed this way, proof positive that I was beyond Watford, and now in what government calls 'the regions', where the only way to make a business pay is arson. My depression returned, I went back to the noisy womb of the pub.

Next morning, breakfast was substantially larger than any meal I had eaten for three days. Admittedly, my efforts at self-catering had resulted in dishes that would not have been out of place in a Gandhi cook-book, but it is still always a pleasure to see a plate with standing room only. The main cause for this largesse were the landlady's regulars; all long-distance lorry-drivers, and all, as I soon saw, with a calorie intake that roughly matched the fuel consumption of a 36 tonner. They were a cheery group, but the realisation that, if they tak'd the high road *or* the low road, they'd still be in Scotland a fortnight afore me, did not lighten my step. Nor did the conversation of three would-be young Army officers, self-fancying Action Men, who, despite the absence of any war, had yomped it from Edale to the pub in under twelve hours the previous day. Faced with this information, I claimed to have taken the scenic route. I noted with some satisfaction that they did not appear to be feeling too well. To help with their training, I offered to sit in one of their packs for the next twenty-four hours.

And then it was time to be off and up again. It was not so much the call of the wild any longer, more a ritual as remorseless and depressing as catching the 8.23 every morning. And just like the commuter whose car coughs and splutters all the way to the station, so, too, I had a body whose parts rarely worked from cold. Not being fitted with a choke, I always had to begin the day by kick-starting each leg, repeatedly. I jerked slowly back up the track to the moors.

The true test of wilderness lies in that sense of not only being alone, but of being the first there . . . of having to cut back the grass for when Adam and Eve arrive later. Seeing as, within the first twenty miles of Yorkshire, you come across seven major roads and a stationary hot dog van, this feeling is hard to sustain. Indeed, the state of the climb to Blackstone Edge suggests that Hannibal and his elephants have just gone past – closely followed by municipal wilderness officers hammering down several miles of raised wooden footways, as the path is now so hopelessly eroded that it makes a wider gash in the hillside than the M62 which it crosses. Trudging through the endless gobbets of post-Marsden moor, and knowing that below me were two railway tunnels and Britain's largest canal tunnel, I felt definitely short-changed on the born-free element of the walk. If I was going to die of exposure I thought it unheroic to do so within sight of a bus route.

Nonetheless, despite being sniffy about the intrusiveness of man, I did find time for Arnie's aforementioned hot dog van. But, welcome though it was beside the track, a true entrepreneur would have recognised a prime site for a hearse and done a roaring trade in dead walkers. Nearby, but more mysteriously, stood a police car, presumably keeping an eye out for walking infringements. I bought a cup of tea and gazed at the GPO's less-than-rural giant wireless masts next door.

It was late morning on my first day in the North; a battered Marina arrived, the driver opened the back door and out came two children, opened the boot and out came two dozen racing pigeons – all apparently with a 1 p.m. appointment in Hebden Bridge – and then the family got back in and drove off. No-one batted an eyelid or handed out a Tourist Board brochure. Being a socially progressive walker, I always avoid thinking in stereotypes and have never been Northist in my attitudes. I had another cup of tea and waited for the arrival of the clog-dancers and the tripe salesmen.

All that arrived was another walker. (You can never find one when you want one.) We teamed up – he said he was in no hurry – and together we successfully crossed the M62 footbridge. A young man, his face twitched with contempt at the sight of the cars hurtling senselessly along below us. I too felt disapproval of the cars, but only to the extent that I wasn't in one of them. Still, I kept carefully quiet about my views on the internal combustion engine as the Ramblers' Association can be rather strict on unnatural desires. Nonetheless, after a morning of long-distance lorries, turbo-charged pigeons, and now high-speed saloons, I began to think that being a biped was some form of design fault.

Next on the map it says Redmires – and this is not a cartographer's whimsy. But even if slime came in multi-coloured patterns, like seaside rock and children's tooth-paste, it would still have a major public relations problem with me. For once, however, the struggle brought a reward: arrival at Blackstone Edge, on 'the Andes of England' as Defoe put it. It was virtually the end of Stage

MAP 3: SECT. C

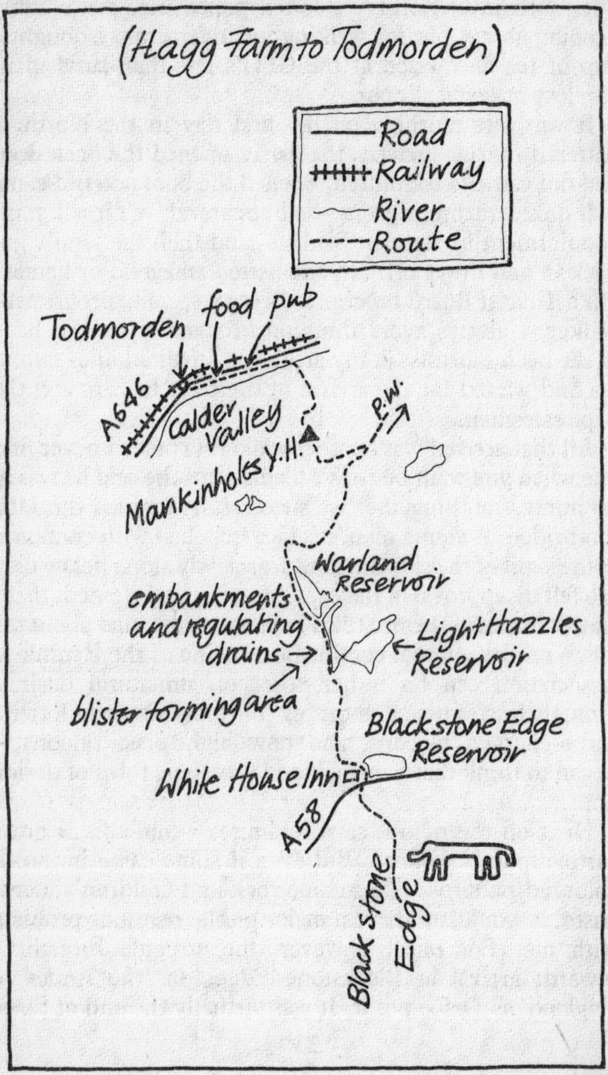

(Hagg Farm to Todmorden)

Road
Railway
River
Route

Todmorden   food pub
A646   Calder Valley   P.W.
Mankinholes Y.H.
Warland Reservoir
embankments and regulating drains
Light Hazzles Reservoir
blister forming area
Blackstone Edge Reservoir
White House Inn   A58
Black stone Edge

One and the start of life without gaiters. Upon Blackstone Edge it was almost touristy; it had not rained all morning – an event which makes local farmers behave as though the Sahara were about to open a second front – and also a rather good view had been made available. (I could nearly see Stoodley Pike in the distance.) So, instead of stopping to rest on our mud-encrusted laurels, Richard and I decided to press on three miles to celebrate at The White House Inn, one of the very rare pubs en route. It does food. Unfortunately, it called 'Time!' some 30 seconds before we arrived. Already Stage Two seemed rather reminiscent of Stage One.

After Blackstone Edge the walking is definitely firmer, mainly because the local authorities have managed to persuade some of the loose water to live in reservoirs . . . Blackstone Edge Reservoir, Light Hazzles Reservoir, Warland Reservoir. It is a dispiriting sight – seeing water in a reservoir is somehow like seeing a wild animal in a zoo. Water should be *doing* things, like drowning people, or jumping off rocks, or even just making your drink fizz, but up here in the Pennines all it does is lie around in concrete, moping, until someone turns a tap on in Manchester. So, for mile after flat, high mile, along waterworks road and regulating drain, embankments and cinder paths, the landscape becomes a dispiriting hybrid of bleak but not wild, empty but not virgin. (I could see Stoodley Pike in the distance.)

There are few things more depressing than such a trek. One of them is such a trek with Richard. In earlier centuries, world travellers appear as colourful, larger-than-life adventurers, prone to bring back an extra country or two to add to the monarch's collection. In the well-ordered late twentieth century, the people who wander restlessly round the globe are the ones who have lost their P45s; behaving with disregard for the future is now deviant, not buccaneering, and he who sails the seven seas burns his boats (modern Jobcentre motto). And so it was with Richard. He was about 30, and at present putting tins on supermarket shelves. He was just back, he said, from Peru . . . or Malaysia . . . or Nepal . . . or somewhere. (They all look alike, these foreign places.) He was shortly to leave again, for good, to earn his fortune in Brazil . . . or Malawi . . . or somewhere. He had obviously seen Judy Garland sing 'Somewhere Over the Rainbow' and mistaken it for Careers Advisory Information set to music. And yet he travelled not so much hopefully as apathetically; his decision to live abroad had all the chill glamour of exile. At 40, he would, I suspected, be putting tins on foreign supermarket shelves. And not long after that, be putting 'dosser' on his passport.

I think I was the most depressed by the way he carried his roots on his back. For me, the desolation of the moors had been as much a test of identity as physique (and I had failed both). The empty featureless expanses had found my spirit not so much unquenchable as self-extinguishing. Within six hours of setting off, a desire for home, hearth, wife, pipe, slippers and two labradors had set in – and this despite having no dogs and being a non-smoking, unmarried, short-term tenant with central heating (the slippers were fortunately part of my 3 cwt. baggage allowance). I had long wanted to be an explorer. But I now feared that if I ever tried to circumnavigate the globe I would find my umbilical cord so firmly knotted to civilisation that I could not get past Dover. For Richard, home was where the sleeping bag was, and that inspired in me a mixture of envy and panicky terror.

These comments might give the impression that, on a merely physical plane, life, though difficult, was not a major problem. This would be an error. All but the most alert of GPs would have authorised burial. Previously, the one good result from having a million years of compressed sponges underfoot was that I had been without blisters. Now, with the arrival of easy hard going they had found their natural habitat. Soon I had more water under the skin than is found in the average family-sized bog. I also found I had Richard under the skin. And the sun was getting tired as well. The route seemed to stretch ahead for miles along the plateau (I could clearly see Stoodley Pike in the distance), following the Calder Valley and eventually dropping down into it near an outcrop of sandals and bushy beards known as Hebden Bridge, the Liberal H.Q. for revivalist macrobiotics. It was a daunting prospect, and one I allowed Richard to tackle alone.

Flagging fast, I made a decision; or, to be more exact, an error of judgment; or, to be scrupulously pedantic, a total cock-up. I decided to call it a day, and drop steeply down the nearest part of the valley to Mankinholes Youth Hostel. Let us leave aside the fact that, like Yin and Yan, for every descent there is an equal and opposite ascent; let us also leave aside that such diversions add extra-curricular miles to the journey and an aching hour to two waking days; let us instead concentrate on the fact that Mankinholes Youth Hostel is closed on Wednesdays.

The A646, which runs along the Calder Valley, has many features – a sewage works, a disgusting canal, a dubious river, a railway line, a pig farm, and large speeding lorries. All it was short of, at 8 o'clock that Wednesday night, was a bed. Or another human being. I shuffled despairingly along the deserted pavements, now in real pain. As pus built up in my foot, so vitriol built up in my spleen. I made a draft proposal that the Calder Valley be declared an Area of Outstanding Unnatural Ugliness; I drew up a binding contract offering the whole for free toxic waste disposal – on the grounds that no one would notice the difference; and I swore a great deal. I do not know the exact compass bearing of my route, but it could be roughly described as in the direction of mid-Wales.

It was not until the outskirts of Todmorden that I finally found an unwilling pub landlord. Guests were clearly not his speciality. The bar was empty, the larder was bare, and the bedroom had no soul. There is a type of wallpaper only bought to be put in rooms that one will never inhabit oneself. It is probably much in demand for the set of Huis Clos. There is also a type of furniture so tacky that it must have begun life second-hand. And it usually ends life

Best room? Its our only room.

untaken even at the Scouts Jumble Sale. Together, this wallpaper and this furniture, they live in lonely rooms where the windows never open, just rattle, and where the pipes never flow, just gurgle. And where the lonely walker feels sorry for himself.

It took a further half-mile of blood, sweat and blisters to find dinner. It was microwaved pie and chips in a cavernous, modernised bar, where a smile clearly cost extra. Customers were few. There was the odd youth, the odd bird, the occasional flirtatious obscenity. The most life came from the one-arm bandit. Wednesday was obviously not a big night in Todmorden. I went back to my room. I greatly missed Richard.

4 A GIANT LIMP FOR MANKIND

I got out of the valley as I got in – by courtesy of a nineteenth century philanthropist. In the early 1800s, there was a Lancashire Cotton Famine that did to the local economy the same unmentionable acts which the 1970s Oil Crisis did to half the globe. It is thought a modern heretical solution to pump money into the mysterious world of the infrastructure, but here over 150 years ago one Honest John Fielden did just that, and pumped his spare groats into paying the unemployed to build a quite unwanted private carriageway to take him up from his castle in the valley to Stoodley Pike (which he could no doubt see in the distance). He was that rarity, a Keynesian millowner. But even had he been an ardent monetarist, or a white-slave trafficker, I would still have welcomed his firm, flat flagstones. They bore a startling resemblance to the surface conditions which, before leaving home, I had expected to find supplied as standard issue for each of the 270 miles.

The Stoodley Pike monument, which I could now see in 120 foot close-up, also has a noble origin. It was erected in 1814 to celebrate peace (or: How They Brought The Good News From Ghent To The West Riding). Like Keynesian economics, such acts are now out of favour – any large government structures stuck upon hillsides today are usually there to help start a war, not commemorate the ending of one. Nor are they exactly of homogeneous local materials. Stoodley Pike is not, of course, inconspicuous – I gained the distinct impression it was on wheels, and got moved around Yorkshire to impress the maximum number of tourists – but it does have a certain defaced grandeur.

MAP 4: (DAY 5)

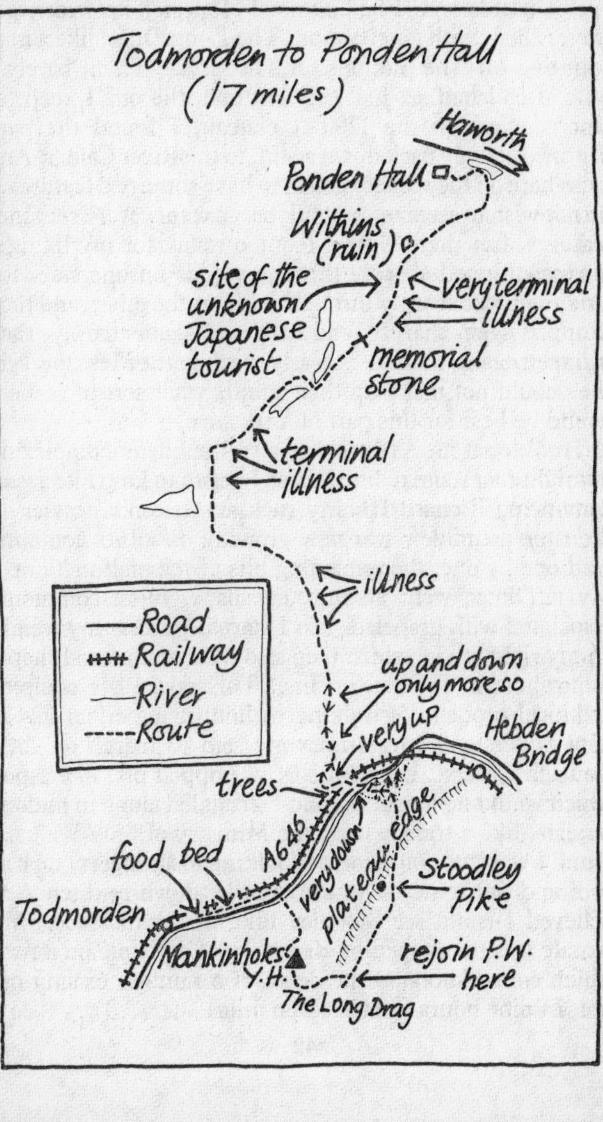

Todmorden to Ponden Hall
(17 miles)

Haworth

Ponden Hall □

Withins
(ruin) ○

site of the
unknown
Japanese
tourist → ← very terminal
← illness

memorial
stone

terminal
illness

illness

up and down
only more so

Hebden
Bridge

very up

trees

food bed

A646

very down

plateau edge

Stoodley
Pike

Todmorden

Mankinholes
Y.H. ▲

rejoin P.W.
here

The Long Drag

Legend	
——	Road
+++	Railway
——	River
----	Route

Unfortunately, having reached it, the more delicate of my own features were feeling vandalised.

I had awoken, that fifth morning, with a definite shortage of usable feet. I had climbed Honest John's carriageway, called, with good reason, The Long Drag, like a man counting off The Stations Of The Cross. Then, barely a mile after I had set foot (my left one, the one I keep for emergencies) on the 1200 ft plateau, I found the path dropped steeply back down again, to the River Calder. And from here on the scenery began to have some real features. I do not wish to seem ungrateful, because they were very nice features, but there were a few too many for my liking – having dropped sharply through woods on one side, the land then rose sharply through fields on the other, and then dropped again sharply, and then rose again sharply, then dropped again, then . . . Clearly, back in the Mesozoic age, they could not make up their minds what sort of scenery would be best for this part of Yorkshire.

Trouble set in. As I tried to give the blister complex on my right foot room to breathe, so I began to limp like a very convincing Richard III. My rucksack became heavier all the time as mildew was now growing on all its contents. And one by one, the remaining bits of me malfunctioned. My left knee went an unusual shape, more commonly associated with grapefruit, so I started putting my weight on my right ankle, which then also went an unusual shape, somewhere in the balloon line. This raised the complex technical problem of walking without using either leg. (I now understood why armies are said to march on their stomachs.) Next, my boot sort of popped off, like a pod which would no longer fit, and I struggled along in undone sandals, like a trainee from the Ministry of Silly Walks. I found I was stopping a lot, and talking to strangers, such as bees and butterflies. I would even lie down in ditches. (I believed I could see Stoodley Pike in the distance.) My morale was not helped by discovery of a plaque on a rock which commemorated the death of a rambler exactly my age. In nine hours I made seven miles.

I was lying full length under the setting sun – with a weather eye open for vultures – when a solitary Japanese gentleman, in the regulation tourist black suit, Bri-Nylon shirt and matching camera accessories, leant over me. He pointed to a stone ruin some 50 yards away and said, 'Is Blonte?' Is Blonte? I nodded encouragingly – always the best approach – and he and his lens zoomed off.

And then I realised I was in Wuthering Heights country. I felt a novel stir within me and staggered to my knees. Half a stony mile below lay Ponden Hall, alias Thrushcross Grange. It has beds. An hour later, I was at the door, enquiring the price of a night, when I observed it also has rather splendid architecture. In particular, I noticed the flagstones as I crashed headlong to the ground.

Ponden Hall had a large open fire. It also had regular filling meals. And it had a number of motherly, middle-aged women on a weaving course. For two whole days I sat by the fire, I ate the meals, I made myself available for mothering. I felt like a World War I veteran home from the front. (I did have competition – Richard was in the next armchair, sporting blisters and temporarily unavailable for world tours. But it was generally agreed that none of his blisters was as impressive as my ankle, which, had it been a cabbage, would have won a rosette in a vegetable show.) If the setting was atmospheric seventeenth century, the hospitality was nostalgic 1960s. With the style laid back but all home comforts laid on, the communal eating, communal foot-warming, and communal sleeping (within reason), helped give to the old house a vague flavour of the lost hippy empire. The walls were free from house rules and copies of the Offences Against The Landlady Act; the bathroom had no list of 101 items, including urine, which must not be put down the toilet; and a gentle, pervasive informality reigned.

Hosts and guests all sat down together each night to dine along one great table, and converse. It was an instructive

44

experience. The theory of strangers breaking home-made bread together is a fine one. Unfortunately, it is a practice ill-suited to the English. For the English to become well-acquainted requires at least 30 years of marriage; a meal, even of four courses, is in no way enough to produce an exchange of views. To the French and Italians, a meal is a real social occasion, but to the English the food is merely there as a potential obstacle to good table manners. And so each night, when faced with, among others, a bearded libertarian, a Manxman with a Messianic faith in the birch, a government adviser on foreign aid, more than one highly-sexed weaving divorcee, a world traveller, and a writer, we merely praised the cooking and passed the salt. We talked of cabbages but no kings. Our digestive juices warned us that if minds met, they might meet head-on – and DISAGREEMENT could occur, which would embarrass us. It is a peculiar trait of this country that expressing an opinion is seen as the intellectual equivalent of flashing.

The daylight hours were more self-indulgent. Almost sunk out of sight on the sofa, it was a rare chance to read piles of old magazines without the imminent arrival of a dentist. As I sat and read and throbbed, and advised the occasional enquirer about the finer points of long-distance walking, I felt my status revive a little nearer to quo. I even had a kit inspection, although, given the respective states of the kit and myself, it could more easily have come and inspected me.

On the second afternoon, a nice, kind lady drove me into nearby Haworth, that I might see the pretty cobbled streets and wave at the Bronte coach-trippers and buy some Bronte postcards. The tourist board should pay royalties. There can be few literary sites that receive a larger public – apart, of course, from Dante's Inferno. Even Ponden Hall received its share of literary fanatics, often women strangely obsessed by the novels, who behaved as though spurned personally by Heathcliff. Wuthering Heights must be one of those rare set texts that can claim to have groupies.

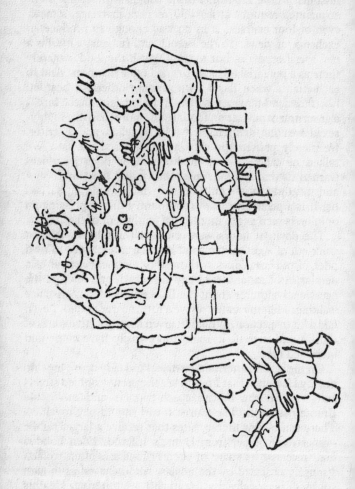

My close study here was of maps. I was carrying ten. There is a point in every travel book where the author professes a love of maps. This is that point. I love maps. I love the way every last detail fails to correspond to any conceivable feature in the immediate (or, indeed, distant) vicinity; I love the way hours of examination are followed by almost total absence of recall the moment the map is folded up; and I love the way a fully-opened map is, even in a breeze Force 2, the only foolproof method of achieving manned flight so far discovered. I do, however, have just one modest improvement to suggest for maps: an automatically-operated, illuminated, mobile arrow, saying 'You Are Here', as is provided in Tube stations.

The growing air of unreality was seductive. I found myself carpeting the flagstones with maps less as a springboard to action then as a substitute for it. A week had gone by, and with it 53 miles; two weeks and 215 miles remained, or, broken down, (which is how I would be) fifteen miles per day, every single day. As my body grew stronger, so my will grew weaker. They say great civilisations decay when life gets soft; so it was with me. As people sink into the snow and give up, so I was tempted to sink further into the sofa and do likewise. I even prepared a speech in the style of Captain Oates: 'I am not going outside and I may be some time.' I wondered if a B & B sick-note would be recognised as official by friends.

With occasional P.W. hopefuls dropping in – if not dropping out – news from the front filtered through on the bog telegraph – progress reports, comments on form, last known positions of, bequests, etcetera. The news item that gave me most pleasure was the withdrawal of the Action Men, the macho-marchers from Marsden; they had apparently yomped off for an early bath. A grandmother of theirs had died, they reportedly said, and stricken by grief they had all gone home on Day Two. Their legs may not have been officer material, but their powers of imagination would not have disgraced an Army propaganda unit. I wished I had been ruder when we met.

Richard was the next to crack, or, in his case, to burst. His blisters were terminal, he announced, and enquired about the establishment's weekly rates.

Paradoxically, all this news gave me a glimmer of encouragement. I tried to remember my Aesop. I was clearly a dead ringer for the tortoise, but I could not exactly remember how he had beaten the hare. Had he shot it, or had the hare got knackered? Whatever the inside story, I started to fancy myself in the role of tortoise and began to tentatively flex a few tortoise muscles. I still, however, thought I had the insuperable handicap of two sub-standard legs – until I was told that the Pennine Way has, in fact, been completed by a man with just the one leg (not hopping, I was glad to hear, but on specially-adapted crutches). I sensed my moral options were narrowing, but part of me still hoped my physical options were closed.

But on the morning of the eighth day I found the boot fitted the foot; I felt like a very reluctant Cinderella. I also felt in need of a very fit Prince Charming. The main difference between modern exploration and eighteenth century exploration is the telephone, so I rang a tough old Northern friend in Lancaster and sold him the joys of long-distance walking. I did not mention his duties would include being guide, pacemaker, windshield, bog-tester, Sherpa-in-chief and quite possibly pall-bearer, and we arranged to meet 50 miles further on in Hawes.

5 THE PURITAN WALK ETHIC

To my surprise, I was a born-again walker. The slopes were gentle, the weather was kind, and most of the next 25 miles, to Malham through meadows and beside rivers, were a joy. To paraphrase Wordsworth, when Nature pulls the stops out, the sap rises right up your boots. Yes, Arcadia! There were birds I had never seen before, birds that were clearly not sparrows; there were wild flowers so lovely that even paraquat would get a guilty conscience; and, most especially rustic, all those pieces of meat one sees hanging up in butchers had here been assembled into whole animals, moving about. There was also a suspiciously large number of people now claiming to be walking the Pennine Way. You could spend twenty-four hours in a bog and see nobody, nothing but the odd bone, but along the Aire valley there was a waiting list to get over each stile.

It was the Sunday rambler. Like the Sunday driver, they clog the paths, always walking in slow-moving packs and constantly stopping to look at views – or to picnic! Personally, I feel that if people wish to malinger outdoors, they should do it in public parks, away from us professional walkers. This attitude is, of course, jealousy. 'Doing the Pennine Way' requires a timetable as rigorous as any on a package tour; fall behind schedule and you have nowhere to park yourself at night. If tentless, the walking has to be relentless, and this is probably the least satisfying aspect of the whole trek. An inner courier keeps you moving ever onwards, allowing you slightly less time for the wonders of nature then you would normally spend on the calls of nature.

SLOW DOWN
STILE AHEAD

Sunday rambling, on the other hand, has a lovely, old-fashioned quality – as do many of the ramblers. It is a simple pleasure: the nature-lover turns up with the basic five senses, and Nature provides the raw materials. If this happens in Yorkshire, it is usually love at first sight, sound, smell, touch and even taste. Not far from the village of Lothersdale I fell among ramblers, three generations of the same family, for whom the country code ran in the blood. They had a walk for every weather, a view for every season; true non-sophisticates, to them the 'happy hour' was just after dawn. Already, at ten years old, the youngest was able to identify sixteen different brands of tree leaf (even when twenty, all that *I* could tell from a tree's leaves was whether it was winter or not; and even then I had to exclude the complicating factor that the tree might be dead) and quite probably he could recite the law of trespass in his sleep. For a delightful half-hour we all rummaged (this may not be the correct naturalist expression) in the hedgerows, to help compile a check-list of that day's available flora. To a townie, it was a revelation – quite clearly it is not just lily-of-the-valley that has got the edge over K.Solomon.

As a result, for several days afterwards I harboured the idea of becoming a wild-flower buff. I quickly rejected the alternatives of doing birds or animals. Nature study is basically the non-criminal branch of the police force, depending, as it mainly does, upon detection and identification, and the great advantage of a flower is that it does not move around a lot; both birds and animals have unhelpful lifestyles, often wearing camouflage or only going out shopping at night. Since the enthusiast is always being told to take the identification key to the object and not vice versa, I felt the logistics of taking my Observer Book of Birds 200 ft up in the air to check out any unidentified flying objects were all but insoluble. The obvious, commonsense, method, of shooting each creature dead to find out what model it was, seemed a wasteful approach to the subject. So I opted for flora.

My disillusion with flowers began when I realised that

each one had about as many close, not to say indistinguishable, relatives as the average Heinz bean. I had envisaged being au fait with the rarer orchids in about a fortnight at the outside; it came as a great setback to learn that even the common-or-garden (I use the term in its more precise seventeenth century sense, of course) daisy, with which I had thought myself on intimate terms since kindergarten, had a family daisychain covering over 45 full pages of my modest little beginner's guide. As far as I could see, most species miscegenated with the frequency of floral rabbits, and so completing a positive I.D. on any flower in the short space of summer would appear a work of Kew-like genius. But the real body-blow to my amateur naturalist phase came when I lost my innocence about grass itself. Grass is grass is grass (and, occasionally, possibly, is cannabis) I had trustingly thought. Yet that ordinary-looking, green, wavy stuff, seemingly worth a Design Centre Award for simplicity, comes in every known, and indeed unknown, size, shape, sheath, stamen, stigma, stem, tuft, tussock, floret, spikelet, panicle, ligule, glume, node, nodule, bract, blade and sexual orientation available. In fact, it comes in more varieties than there are botanists to study it. Even the Latin takes eight years of Open University courses. I decided to postpone my botany – after all, given the speed at which mankind is starting to destroy the world's vegetation cover, by the year 2010 there will probably only remain one purpose-built uniflower, and then we can all be expert naturalists.

Hedgerow duty done, the rambling family fell victim to a 'Cream Teas' sign outside a farm. Sadly, I was already several fields behind schedule and so, driven on by the Puritan walk ethic, I said my second goodbyes of the morning; parting was sweet, if not creamy, sorrow. But Sunday was unremitting temptation, the countryside was booby-trapped with pleasures: hay-making to watch, larks to listen to, trees to lie under. And then after 'the happy wanderers' came 'messing about in boats'. In the afternoon, near East Marton, the path followed the Leeds and

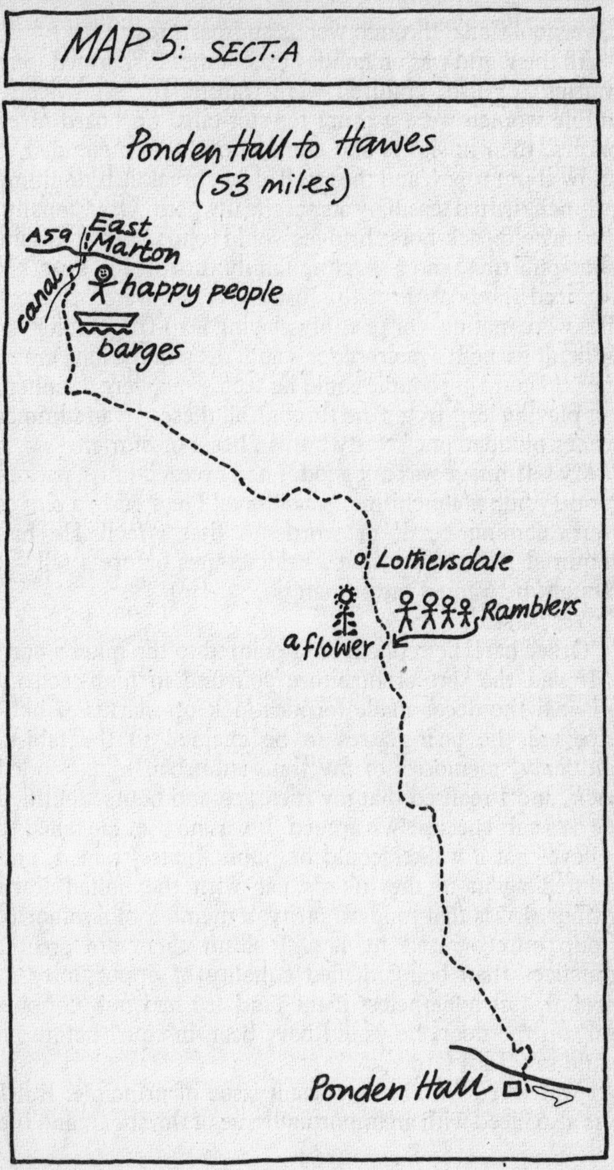

MAP 5: SECT·A

Ponden Hall to Hawes
(53 miles)

A59 East Marton
canal
happy people
barges

Lothersdale
a flower
Ramblers

Ponden Hall

Liverpool Canal through woods and pastures.

All the world was on holiday except me. Fishermen were waiting for fish, children were waiting for sandwiches, nubile women were waiting for sun-tans; on board hired barges, men in shorts and commodore hats pretended to know about ropes, and the smell of late breakfasts doubling as lunch drifted teasingly across the towpath. Occasionally, the tiny old pack-horse bridges would echo to a boat-engine phut-phutting, and a giggling family tut-tutting, as father bounced the boat through. Just above the water, dragon-flies were mating – or possibly playing leap-frog; biology is difficult without a microscope – and, deep in the long grass, the odd courting couple could be seen, who were definitely not playing leap-frog. And through all these sylvan summer scenes plodded one sweaty human beast of burden.

My self-image was not good. I had breezed into a packed country pub at lunchtime. 'Landlord!' I had said, 'a pint of your foaming best!' or words to that effect. He had enquired if I was a walker. Pride comes before a fall – I thought he wanted my autograph.

'Yes,' I said.

'Other bar!' he replied. And pointed to the hiker's bar.

It had the sort of furniture you find in high-security prisons; the decor made formica look up-market. I half-expected the beer-glasses to be chained to the tables. Suddenly, memories of my trans-suburban hike flooded back, and I realised that my rucksack and boots identified me as a sub-species. We argued. It was no use. He failed to believe that a walker could be public-house-trained, and pointed again to the hiker's bar with the bolted-down fittings. I was that modern rarity, a member of a minority group unrecognised by law. I admit there are greater injustices than being denied equality of opportunity to alcohol, but nonetheless if the landlord had put 'Gippo's Bar' on the door, he would have been in court before he could say 'Last Orders!'

I was faced with an important issue of principle. But I was also faced with an important issue of thirst . . . and the knowledge that 'to take my custom elsewhere' would take four hours. I swallowed my pride and beer and joined a little knot of social rejects. As we sat, once mighty walkers, now sullenly huddled together, and clustered forlornly over our Ordnance Survey maps, we looked to all the world like inmates planning a mass break-out. My sense of grievance was heightened by the type of clientèle in the non-hiker's bar. They were the Sunday gin and Jag set, all dressed in the sneakers and cashmere sweaters of the ersatz walking brigade. They were the sort of people who dress up to go for a drive to look at a walk. And my pique, as I watched them walk on carpets and place their bums on soft upholstery, sprang from being aware that, inch for Gore-Tex inch, foot for woolly tartan foot, I was almost certainly the most expensively-dressed person in the entire pub.

By way of over-compensation, I spent the night in the luxury of a Category 4 Guest House, in Gargrave.

Gargrave is a pretty village, divided delightfully by the Aire, and noxiously by the A65. Only two events of note occurred. As I hobbled with evening rigor mortis to collect a take-away, an old-age pensioner stopped me in the street, and enquired, as one equal to another, after my health. And secondly, next morning I had to put off leaving until the bank opened – because I had not enough money to pay for the extravagant gesture of the night before.

It was ominously late, gone 10 a.m., when I left. The riverside bank and its meadows grew progressively lovelier, and my only complaint, as a consumer, was the excessive number of stiles. I would like, if I may, to say a word or two about stiles. They have a design fault – quite apart from being deliberately made two inches narrower than your rucksack. When you raise your right leg – an activity which, in my condition, required a fork-lift truck – this causes your centre of gravity to be unhelpfully relocated at the back of your rucksack, so that any consequent lifting of the left leg (the other one) leaves you tipped unneatly backwards and hanging as though at an audition for the role of three-toed sloth in a David Attenborough series. A day

55

of climbing over stiles is almost as exhausting as a day of pot-holing through bogs. Therefore – although the official handbooks on rambling do tend to be a bit sniffy about this approach on purist grounds – I myself, when tackling stiles, always recommend the use of the Mills hand-grenade bomb.

At last I came upon proof that the scenery really was superb: dozens of tourist coaches blocking the view. Malham has the misfortune to be both beautiful and accessible. So many tourists were wandering around the village that I had the suspicion it might have been built by Disney. But with this misfortune comes a fortune. I think even the telephone kiosk did bed and breakfast, and in some tea-shoppes you have to pay extra *not* to eat cream teas; it is a wonder the farm tractors don't carry ice-lollies and play chimes. Here, the tourist is as well-targeted as the grouse. The area is so wonderfully photogenic that even the local sheep seem to have gone into modelling.

I had done the tourist rounds of Gordale Scar and Janet's Foss several times before, and so I pressed onwards, though feeling slightly philistine about it, and wanting a rucksack sticker saying 'We have already seen the sights of Malham.' What I had not seen before was the daily tourist ritual in front of the spectacular cliffs at Malham Cove. It was to be my finest hour.

The wall-to-wall coaches had unloaded batches of pink, perspiring persons who floundered about on the gentle approach slopes, squealing and puffing helplessly. After years of bodily abuse and abandon, they could no more go uphill than water. Firing on half a lung and supported by honorary legs only, each stumbled to a pre-cardiac collapse, and fell down in gasping heaps. It was a shameful sight. If the events in the Book of Genesis are ever rerun, large sections of the human population would fail to qualify as a species suitable for survival on land. I came into my own. In a move later to be known as The Hiker's Revenge, I strode rhythmically through their midst, head erect, nose slightly retroussé. In a burst of smug superiority and fluid

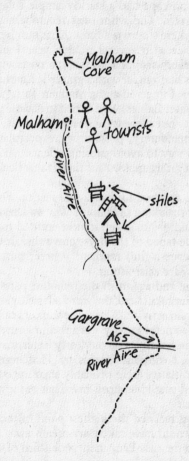

MAP 5: SECT. B

(Ponden Hall to Hawes)

Malham Cove ←

Malham

River Aire

tourists

stiles

Gargrave
A65 →

River Aire

hip movement, I accelerated on and up, away and over the top with that bouncy spring in the step that comes from the first sign of a protruding nail in the boot.

Underfoot now was limestone, a sensible, properly-drained sort of rock, which would provide near-perfect walking conditions were it not that the holes down which the water drains were all too frequently walker-size. The new landscape had a starkly simple colour-scheme: white and green. The white was recumbent rock, lying loose everywhere (there is a limit to the number of walls you can build, even in several million years) and the green was impeccably-cropped grass ('It's no bovver wiv a hovver, but it's like a razor with a grazer'). And there was blue sky, all over. I lingered along Malham Tarn (the inspiration for The Water Babies), and I tried to dawdle through its nature reserve, but there were so many notices, advisory, regulatory, mandatory, prohibitory, expostulatory, that I could see no way to avoid causing offence, short of becoming a bird or a rare moss. And then it was back to gritstone and bog.

As I climbed to over 2,100 feet on Fountains Fell, the earlier rush hour of Pennine Way walkers ended as abruptly as it had begun. I felt almost entitled to see apologies for absence taped to the dry-stone walls. But even alone there was never a dull moment – here, mine-shafts were the penalty for misrouting.

Time and again, in the remotest parts of the Pennines, one stumbles (I use the word advisedly) over ancient signs of human activity. Where the workers came from, and how – and sometimes why – is a seeming mystery. Perhaps the sites are examples of very early Enterprise Zones, set up in deprived wilderness areas by Thatcherite Romans; serfs with initiative were probably encouraged to develop these isolated small bog firms in exchange for reduced tribute to Caesar.

I had reached the highest point of the walk so far. The view would have taken my breath away if I had had any. Before me rose Penyghent, one-third of The Three Peaks,

MAP 5: SECT. C

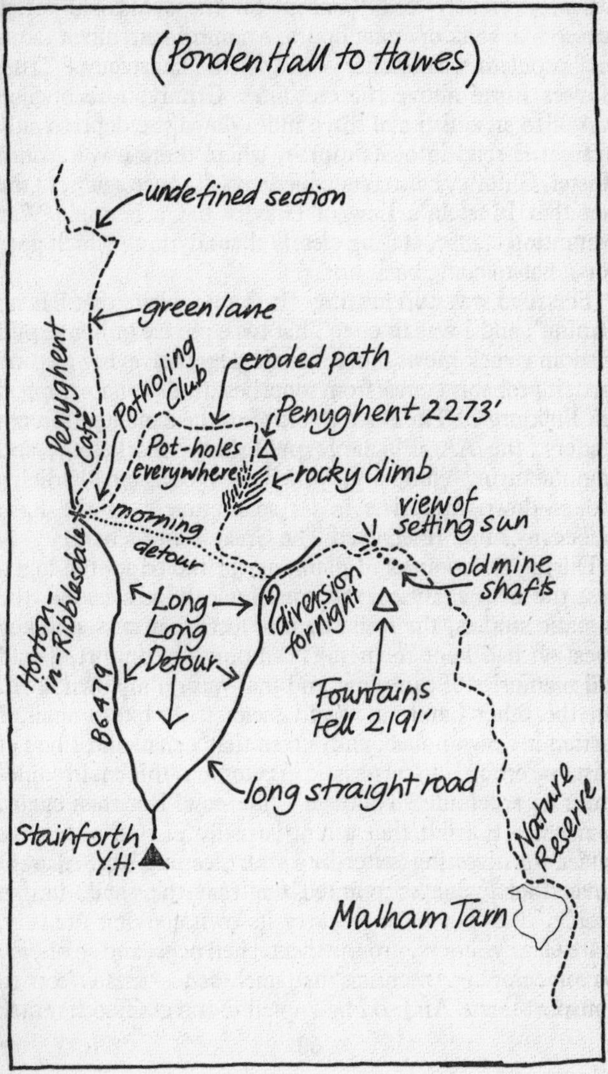

(Ponden Hall to Hawes)

undefined section

green lane

Penyghent Cafe

Potholing Club

eroded path

Penyghent 2273'

Pot-holes everywhere

rocky climb

morning detour

view of setting sun

old mine shafts

Horton-in-Ribblesdale

B6479

Long Long Detour

diversion fortnight

Fountains Fell 2191'

Stainforth Y.H.

long straight road

Nature Reserve

Malham Tarn

silhouetted against the setting sun. I gazed in wonderment – Penyghent I had expected, the setting sun was a complete surprise. All around me lay the majestic countryside of the Dales, gloriously empty except for the occasional vet. I cursed late bank opening hours. An imminent, albeit familiar, problem was arising – to wit, the shortage of Trust Houses Forté above the tree line. Grimly, I reconciled myself to an additional three miles down the depressingly straight B-road into Stainforth, where there was a Youth Hostel. Glumly, I also reconciled myself, once again, to the fact that Einstein's Law of Gravity has a Pennine Way exemption clause, stating clearly that anything which goes down has to come back up.

The road was unremitting. 'It is a long lane that has no turning', and I was in one. That twee phrase of homespun wisdom struck me as more meaningless with every passing yard; it probably comes from some beautifully-photographed AA Folklore Of The Road Book. (For the benefit of foreign readers, the AA is a large publishing, marketing, and manufacturing company, which also occasionally helps broken-down motorists in its spare time.) As the light faded, my mind re-enacted The Great Tent Debate.

During the months of planning for the trip – the logistics, the map analyses, the communications systems, the climatic studies, the research into local dialects – one key question had kept recurring: camping or comfort? I had bad memories of camping, and that was on my own lawn. On the other hand, it would mean that, like a snail, I carried my own house, and, given that a snail and I had at least one crucial characteristic in common, this could sometimes be a definite advantage – like now! But then again, in my heart, I felt that a tent is really just an expensive device for diverting water into your sleeping bag. Also, O Level biology never pointed out that the snail, unlike people, does not have to carry its own cooking utensils, spare Gaz cylinders, groundsheet, shell pegs, and so on; *my* list of camping essentials had included a small Jeep to transport them. And so I had opted to travel smooth rather than rough, to reduce my load and thus increase my speed – a cause-and-effect relationship of which I had seen no evidence since Day One.

It was a wise choice. A familiar and comic sight at Ponden Hall had been grotesquely-overladen campers trying to post Le Creuset saucepans and cutlery trays back to their parents; the second-hand market in unused camping equipment is nowhere finer than along the first 50 miles of the Pennine Way. To spend the days bent double in agony to gain the benefit of nights spent crumpled, cold and insect-chewed is a dubious bargain. And yet, despite everything, I would have paid twice any going rate to a passing tent salesman on that never-ending road that night.

It was nearly dark when I arrived at the hostel. This time, for once, the hostel was not closed, nor was it shut for repairs; it was bursting with lights and life. It was full.

An hour's urgent enquiries revealed that the whole of Yorkshire was full. Not only was there no room at the inn, even the stables were double-booked. At that precise moment, to my gall, every available Dales mattress was in the manicured possession of some pink, perspiring person relaxing after a hard day's coach tour and several hours of intensive tourism.

It was gone midnight when an empty pot-holing club at Horton-in-Ribblesdale was unlocked for me. The evening's climax to a glorious day's walk was not as I had planned. I do not wish to seem ungrateful, but pot-holer's accommodation is clearly designed to toughen them up for potholing. The sleeping area was like open-plan police cells, but without the mod.cons. The bunks were just bare benches, and the temperature was so low that I had to dress for bed. I had also been ten hours without a meal, and the only food available was bread and water without the bread. And what was more, with the lights off, the whole building echoed to strange sounds, easily identifiable as the habits of ghosts and mad axe-men. I was by now exhausted, freezing, starving and close to snivelling. If all this could happen to me in a well-populated English village, it made

me wonder whether my plans for the Amazon the following year were over-optimistic. Getting to sleep that night was the toughest challenge of the walk so far.

I had just managed it when the first pot-holer of the day arrived. It was 5 a.m. I was bleary-eyed and bleary-bodied. We exchanged greetings and I quickly made clear and firm disclaimers to being a pot-holer, for fear lest I be suddenly roped up and taken down a large hole. I have strong views on pot-holing. I regard a pot-hole as the least attractive orifice on earth, and pot-holing has for me the same charm as exploring someone else's nostril with your index finger. It does not surprise me at all that its practitioners wear the sort of rubber gear only found in the seediest of sex shops.

As more and more pot-holers began seeping through the door, I gave the limp arms of Morpheus the elbow, and got up, not that it was a difficult decision. The night had brought back all those bleak teenage memories of trying to sleep on floors after awful teenage parties, except that here the hard boards had not been softened by alcohol, nor had there been the remotest possibility of a grope to keep me warm. Even up, I felt down and out. My body felt unpleasantly coated in grease and grime, as if I had been on British Rail overnight, but since I thought it a more pleasant feeling than the cold shower on offer, I resigned myself to being undesirable for the day. And then I set a new world record for departure times. The rucksack had merely to be picked up, not packed up, and breakfast was equally soon over, there being a limited number of ways to prepare fresh water. I made my excuses, as they say, and left.

No sooner was I outside than I felt unexpectedly enthusiastic, even if blurred in mind and vision. All around lay the dawn, a time of day I had previously only seen in photographs. An envigorating freshness was abroad – were I being trained by Wordsworth, I would have said that the world had been sprinkled with nature's eau-de-cologne – and I felt glad to be alive as I started back, conscientiously, to climb Penyghent from where I had left off. Everywhere, birds were singing, and dew was thick on the ground.

The dew was soon gone – 100 yards on, and it had turned into mist that was thick above the ground, and the birds had all gone to sing elsewhere. By the time I had scrambled my way up the rocks to the 2,273 ft summit, I was rewarded with a view of silent nothing, in every direction. More than miffed, indeed, feeling like a case of virtue kicked in the privates, I hung around for over half an hour; but so did the mist. (I have since been back to Penyghent at least twice and the mist has still not gone.) The journey down was equally depressing – as the Pennine Way backtracks into Horton it creates a deep, wide scar, looking as though the Duke of York has been marching his 10,000 men up and down the hill several times, he too presumably being uncertain what time the mist would clear. More than just a pretty rock-face, Penyghent, with Ingleborough and Whernside, is on the country's fastest-moving, least comfortable package tour, The Three Peaks, and, sadly, parts of the path have become a walking, cycling and running sore. I was ready for bed again.

There have been few days in my life – to be exact, one – when I have had seven miles under my belt before my breakfast got there. It was the only day I have ever had Mars bars with chips (twice). Penyghent Cafe, Horton-in-R, is, however, more than just a cafe; it is a walker filling-station crossed with a gossip redistribution centre, and it does for bedraggled ramblers what The Statue of Liberty was once claimed to do for huddled masses. Its owner is an enthusiast, both about walkers and the landscape. If Peter Bayes' shop had the space, he would probably open a museum of Pennine Way memorabilia, and know the detailed background of every discarded sock. An hour of his company is far more informative than actually walking the Pennine Way, and infinitely preferable. Personally, I never felt the same about my anorak and boots and 35 lb rucksack after hearing his story of the man who walked the entire route in a lounge suit carrying a Co-op plastic bag.

After breakfast, and doing to Mars bars what Ian

Botham does to Shredded Wheat, I started the day for the second time. Ahead – a long, long fifteen more miles ahead – was Hawes and my good friend Aus, who would, I hoped, help me establish the story of the man who did the Pennine Way on piggy-back. Part of the way is along the beautiful old Yorkshire 'green lanes', tucked between dry-stone walls, and once the A1s of the long-distance pack-horse driver; a further part is marked as 'undefined', which is the cartographer's way of enjoying a good laugh at the walker's expense; and yet another part follows an old Roman road, very long and very straight – though why Roman roads should be long and straight is a mystery to me since I have yet to meet an Italian motorist capable of driving in a straight line for more than three yards. Altogether, it was a marvellous high-level trek, with stunning views and driving wind and diving curlews. I felt exhilarated, even if at 1,800 ft there was a wind-chill factor that would have turned most Roman knees the colour of woad.

I met few people; if any were going to Hawes, they had taken the underground. (Ominous wire-fenced caves were frequent sights, each offering forbidden penetration into the bowels of the earth, a singularly appropriate image – given the miles of twisted intestinal passages below ground here – and a venue into which wild Minotaurs would not drag me.) Above ground, by late afternoon I was feeling the loneliness of the long-distance walker, not at all a pedestrian emotion. On these remote tracts, all strangers meet like long-lost brothers, and can squeeze hours of intellectual sustenance out of such matters as a comparative study of bootlaces; and, having met like long-lost brothers, they part with the reluctance of Siamese twins. Therefore to see clearly for miles ahead, and to realise that one's best chance of a good conversation is by meeting a sheep with O Levels, can be depressing. (Worst of all, is to be on trackless peat moors and see that something human this way comes, only to discover, an hour later, that your paths are not crossing. This means that one of you is lost. It may be days before you discover which one.)

MAP 5: SECT. D

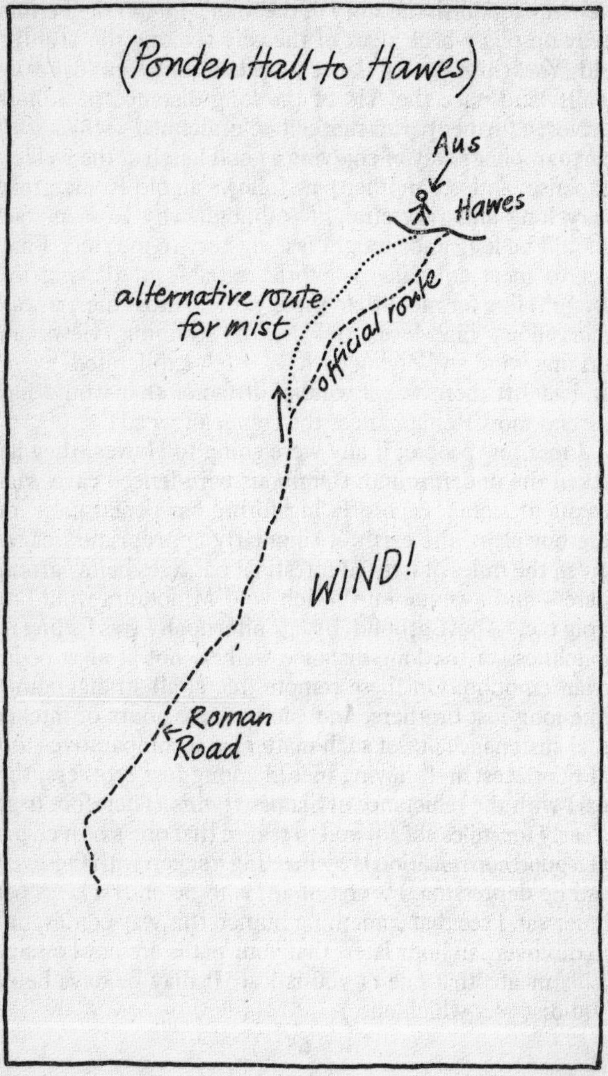

(Ponden Hall to Hawes)

Aus

Hawes

alternative route
for mist

official route

WIND!

Roman
Road

By early evening, the loneliness was worsening, as was the weather. The mist was descending, the miles to go were expanding – and the promise of company, and laughter, and civilised conversation, had the air of an ever-receding mirage. I felt the desolation of an exhausted marathon competitor who fears the crowd will be gone home, and the stadium locked, long before he finishes. So when I finally hobbled into Hawes, sixteen hours after almost waking up, I was not displeased to see Aus.

6 TWO CAN WALK AS SLOWLY AS ONE

Aus (abbrev. for Austin; pron. as in Wizard of Aus; phys. a stocky, muscular Lakelander) was, however, distinctly surprised when he saw me. We had not met for some six months, when I had been twenty years younger. As I lurched from the saloon door to the bar like a Douglas Bader stand-in, a look of incredulity crossed his face, followed closely by uncontrollable laughter. This is not the response Ulysses got from Penelope on his arrival, and it did not, I felt, fully reflect my achievements. Nor did the remark, 'I know some people leave their hearts in San Francisco, but you seem to have left your legs in London!' (More laughter.) Nevertheless, it is a good rule of thumb for effete Southerners not to punch tough Northerners, so I allowed myself a small, only slightly compromising, smile, and accepted a large, highly promising drink.

It was a quiet reunion. Although we had 106 miles of talk to catch up on, my brain was busy catching up on eight hours of sleep. The mist was fast closing in again. I nodded off in mid-ramble several times, and before long it was agreed I should be helped up to bed, stairs being an aspect of civilisation quite beyond my present skills. I seem to remember it was a very comfortable bedroom. No sooner had my feet hit the pillow than I was asleep. I dreamt of pot-holes.

I first realised that our walking partnership could have problems when at breakfast. It had been an unusually — indeed, unprofessionally — late breakfast, and I had noted with concern that Aus not only ordered a second coffee, but lingered over it. He then bought a newspaper to read with it. By the time he had started on the crossword, I harboured doubts that he was familiar with normal walking procedure. I had just decided to officially propose packing, when the suggestion that we spend the morning *shopping in Hawes* confirmed that I was dealing with a hopeless amateur – and one with an apparently retarded metabolic rate.

Hawes is the first proper town of the walk – unless, of course, you are coming from Scotland (a deviant form of walking on which I will comment later). As could be said of almost every town and village in the Dales, it may be small, but it is perfectly-formed. A tourist could spend a very happy hour or two being appreciative of its cobbled streets and old stone buildings. And we did that as well. But it was the men's outfitters that held the principal antiquarian interest. (Key missing parts of Aus's equipment, like gloves, had drawn us in.) In London, men no longer get outfitted, they buy gear; in small market towns, where fashion moves so slowly that it hasn't yet arrived, time and tweed stand still, and the outfitter stands with them. As I stood, and Aus very slowly browsed amidst the clothes, I found myself back in a world where the patterns of life were all solid checks; it was a flare-free land, a land fit for turn-ups, for men big in turnips. Here the clothing trade caters to the man about farm, who outfits himself only on special occasions, usually after world wars, and never appears again except for retreading of cuffs in the event of marriages and deaths. Even the shop's socks, seemingly of a rare yak hair, looked so indestructible that I bought ¾ lb worth, to try and delay that inward advance of my boots first noticed at Malham Cove.

Leaving the shop was not easy. Shopping in the country is a special activity, and if any money changes hands that is just a happy bonus. The Cumbrian in Aus, and the Dalesman in the salesman, meant that the buying of gloves involved more questions and answers than a full-scale MI5 screening. If Aus had needed to buy any other items of clothing, we would have had to rent a cottage for a week.

MAP 6: SECT. A

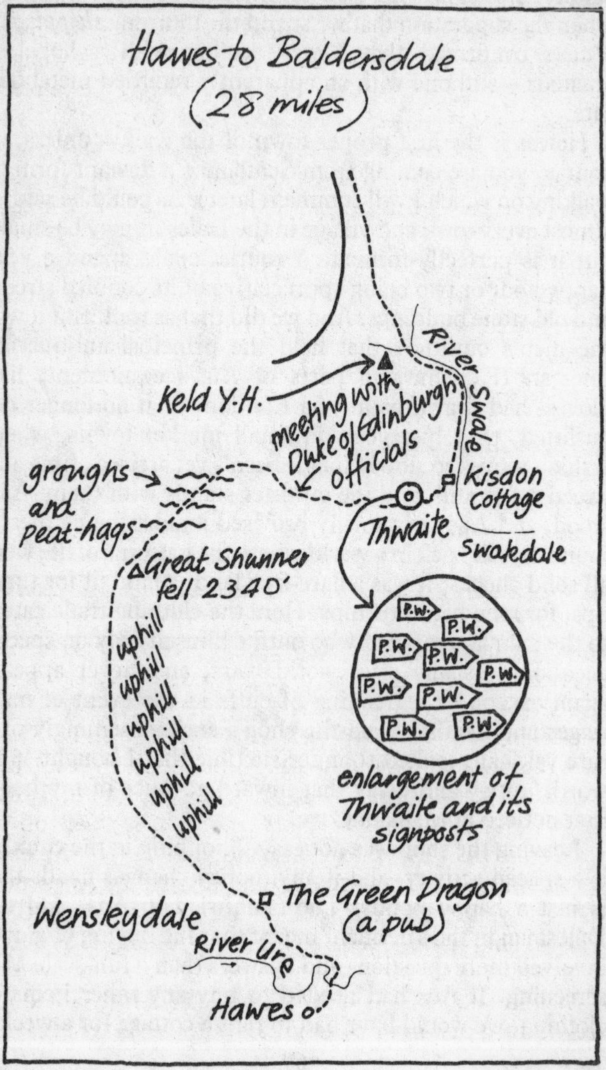

Hawes to Baldersdale
(28 miles)

River Swale

Keld Y.H. → meeting with Duke of Edinburgh Officials

groughs and peat-hags →

kisdon cottage

Thwaite

Swaledale

△ Great Shunner fell 2340'

uphill
uphill
uphill
uphill
uphill
uphill

enlargement of Thwaite and its signposts

P.W. P.W. P.W. P.W. P.W. P.W. P.W. P.W. P.W.

Wensleydale

The Green Dragon
(a pub)

River Ure

Hawes o

We visited several more shops, we may even have admired a church or two, before we finally got out of Hawes. And then, the sky overcast, we set off towards Great Shunner Fell, the mountain of the day. We had gone about a mile, across the meandering River Ure and through the meadows of Wensleydale, and were passing The Green Dragon, a country pub, when Aus suddenly said, 'It's a doddle, this walking, isn't it?' and proposed lunch. I was adamant that we should not stop until later, and said so, firmly, over pie and chips. I kept feeling, as Aus continued chatting happily to the barmaid about her spare time, that I had still not got across to him the essential disciplines of long-distance walking; this belief was strengthened when he suggested waiting in the pub until the weather grew brighter.

Great Shunner Fell is a vast mountain, twenty square miles in area, and with an unbroken (except by death) five miles ascent to its summit at 2,340 feet. I explained patiently to Aus that it is a common misconception among novices that

time req. = miles to be walked ÷ av. walking speed of
4 m.p.h.

and I then went on to further explain that over rough and hilly terrain a realistic speed is usually less than 2 m.p.h. When Aus finally finished his second ice-cream and we did start up Great Shunner Fell, I felt my credibility as senior member of the team was seriously undermined by his maintaining an unbroken and effortless 4 m.p.h. This speed clearly represented an unacceptable state of affairs given that I was a cripple. After much discussion, trial and error, and unsavoury personal abuse, we agreed on a compromise walking system (a modus ambulandi) whereby Aus would walk at his pace, I would walk at my pace, and every 100 yards he would sit down and read a book until I arrived. This arrangement was, however, complicated by the arrival of thick mist, which meant that every 100 yards we were not only lost, but separately lost, and then had to spend a good half-hour shouting and blowing whistles.

71

Fortunately, the re-appearance of my old friends, the groughs, in the company of their close cousins, the peat-hags, helped impose a greater equality on our efforts. And with the onset of steady rain, I felt almost back in my natural habitat, playing, as it were, – or scrummaging – on home territory. Here Aus was invaluable; by allowing him free rein I was able to discover where all the deepest bogs were. Where angels and senior walkers fear to tread, Aus unfailingly rushed in; to find the solid ground, all one had to do was chart a course around him. Happily for me, it took most of the day for him to work out that the shortest distance between two points is usually the deepest.

Nonetheless, it was a miserable, frustrating time – all the way, my guide books gloated on about the 'widespread panoramas' from Great Shunner Fell, and, all the way, the view remained a purely theoretical pleasure. I believe the public mood is now right for the National Parks to fit each of their mountains with a viewpoint in braille.

The great boost to the day's morale came when, emerging at 5 o'clock by the walled lane which descends into Thwaite, we learnt that a crack troop of Duke of Edinburgh gold medallists was missing, presumed bewildered. It was as though I had come of walking age, that at last my day on Kinder Scout had been avenged! Our opinion as master-navigators was sought by two waiting officials, trying hard not to consider the prospect of having to write to parents and offer them replacement children. But we had seen nothing – literally! Our offer to accept honorary medals for our own achievement was turned down, and we moved on into the sunlit joys of Swaledale. (We heard later that the award-scheme party was alive and well and so far away that they could have asked for political asylum in Lancashire.)

It was Dr Johnson who defined a patron as 'one who looks with unconcern on a man struggling for life in the water, and when he has reached ground, encumbers him with help.' So it is with the Pennine Way signpost. On the vast, remote, featureless, treacherous uplands you can struggle for hours and be given no clue, unofficial, official, or divine, as to the route. Arrive down in the village of Thwaite, civilised and safe, and the design and installation of signposts appears to be the principal source of employment. At ten to the mile, it is a wonder they are not joined together with guide-ropes so that the effort of opening one's eyes can be dispensed with altogether. It is a curious and recurring inconsistency. Along some sections of the Pennine Way, I suspect the powers-that-own, having lost the battle to prevent the path's existence, now pursue a policy of benign neglect to prevent the rambler's existence, hoping that, in the countryside absence of the proverbial bus, he, or she, might fall down their mine-shafts or drop over their cliffs. And yet along other sections, unsung heroes have blobbed enough bright yellow dots and arrows to help even the insomniac walker. But in all this, it is the Scot, going South, who is the real pioneer. With typical colonial high-handedness, all the English guidebooks require him to walk backwards.

There is, I hasten to add, more to Thwaite than the sum of its signposts. There are few lovelier villages; there are certainly few that one gets to know more intimately, since the path goes through several gardens and appears to narrowly miss an outside privy.

Nothing much happened on the final section of that day, apart from standard exhaustion, but the three miles from Thwaite to Keld, high on rocky slopes above the upper Swale, require no events to be memorable. I mention these miles for three reasons: firstly, because of their exquisite beauty which has drawn me back time and again since; secondly, because if Kisdon Cottage, with its wonderful views down Swaledale, ever comes on the market, I would like to be notified; and thirdly, because it gave me great pleasure to see Aus was at last beginning to tire, possibly even to limp!

At Keld, we booked our bodies into the Youth Hostel and our clothes into the drying room – we were too late to book for dinner. Although planned as a hostelling holiday,

my management skills had so far caused eight of the twelve nights to be spent elsewhere – indeed, in some cases, anywhere! Yet, on the whole, I had lost little sleep (metaphorically speaking, of course) over this. The English hostel is unique, even though every nation's hostels have their own flavour. In German-speaking Switzerland, my youthful experiences suggested they are run mostly by those ex-members of the Third Reich who could not afford the boat fare to South America; in North Africa, it is not bedding which is laid back but hostellers, and the only smell of cooking is in hash-pipes; in Franco's Spain, 'lights out' used to be enforced by goose-stepping Alsatian dogs, specially-trained by the Guardia Civil to urinate over the bunks of hostellers slow to get into bed; in Greece, by contrast, you need never get out of bed at all, and it can be a problem to prevent the warden from getting in with you. In England, hostels are run by maiden aunts. For maiden aunts . . . Or they were.

A battle is now raging for the soul of youth hostels, fought between the nature-communing purists and the market-oriented modernists. The purists may be on the side of the angels, but the modernists are on the side of the accountants, and accountants usually win. The future may well lie with the mud-free car-walkers, and the credit-card-carrying nature lovers, whose taste for the primitive is limited to Grandma Moses. But maiden aunts take a long time a-dying. And so, out in the rural heartlands, it is still carbolic and curfews; it is still furry blankets, for the folding of, and echoing floors, for the scrubbing of; and it is still an article of faith that, between the hours of 10 and 5, moral fibre only grows outdoors. Somehow, enjoyment of the countryside has become entangled with an archaic, peculiarly English puritanism. It would be churlish to object to the old-fashioned niceness of many a hosteller, but I think it is the 'clean-living' image of youth hostels that makes them somewhat oppressive. A campaign should be mounted at once to persuade the public that a simple love of the countryside is quite compatible with unfettered degeneracy.

Keld itself is a gem – more than one river, more than one waterfall, bundles of orchids, a thousand years of history, and perfect peace. But the less said, the fewer tourists.

There was, however, quite a lot said between me and Aus. We left Keld the same way that we arrived: late. This time he was experimenting with a new method of gaiter-lacing, which had still only reached the prototype stage by 10 a.m. But for once this did not matter too much, as we had set our hearts and stomachs on a drink at the highest pub in England – Tan Hill Inn, 1,732 feet up and four miles on, and more famous for its double-glazing TV advertisements than its beer. Now that the local mines have closed down – or rather, been left open, judging by the warning signs – it is a hideously bleak and lonely spot. The pub stands out, isolated, on the skyline, perched on a watershed to provide target practice for the wind and a last resting place for the mammoth snowdrifts of winter. Arrive at Tan Hill on a frosty night in autumn, and it is quite likely that Last Orders will be called when the snowplough arrives the following Easter. Unfortunately, arrive at lunchtime in June and the quixotic nature of the then-landlord means the doors are bolted, and so, apparently, has he. (Owners here have a faster turn-over than the meat pasties.) All we drank in was the scenery.

A clear view North now lay exposed. In one brief glance was four days' hard labour. Backstage, the eminence grizzly, Fiends Fell (now Cross Fell), highest of the journey's high-points; centre-stage, the unbridged route of the A66, made visible five miles away by the constant flow of high-sided lorries; and here on the apron stage, first and worst, was the evil sludge of Sleightholme Moor, as flat, squelchy and ugly-brown as a cow's giant turd.

For a while, Aus and I sheltered behind the pub wall, facing South to remember past conquests, and hiding from a wind that could overturn a three-ton hiker. (O, to be one of Ted Moult's unruffled feathers inside!) To a casual

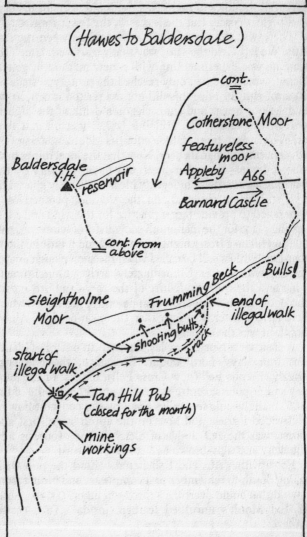

(Hawes to Baldersdale)

cont.

Cotherstone Moor

featureless
moor
Appleby   A66

Baldersdale
Y.H.   reservoir

Barnard Castle

cont. from
above

Frumming Beck   Bulls!

sleightholme
Moor

end of
illegal walk

shooting butts   track

start of
illegal walk

←Tan Hill Pub
(closed for the month)

mine
workings

observer, we were pining for alcohol. To an acute observer, we were pondering on a moral dilemma. All the way from Keld we had scrambled and stumbled up rough, soaking moorland, from which the only sight of note had been a nearby lane running exactly, some would say smugly, parallel to us. The founding fathers of the Pennine Way had a strict code of honour, and so their route goes to elaborate, sometimes labyrinthine, lengths to avoid any immoral liaisons with a classified road; tarmac and concrete come high on their walker's list of forbidden substances. I had remained scrupulously loyal, but immediately ahead were parallel routes of syrup and tarmac, and I was tempted. As I agonised with my conscience – Aus not being averse to even the occasional helicopter – a large party of responsible-looking walkers paused for guidance; when I pointed out the route across the moors, they all said, 'Oh, bugger that!' and went straight down the road.

On my death bed, I may well murmur the words 'Sleight-holme Moor' involuntarily as I expire, leaving loved ones and lawyers with a cryptogram as baffling as Citizen Kane's. But you, gentle readers, will know why, because that day I too went down that minor road – and to this very day still feel as though I indulged in unnatural practices shameful to the name of walker.

Sleightholme Moor is, however, no stranger to unnatural acts. Judging from the old shooting butts, the blasting to death of grouse has long been fun here. Nevertheless, although there is a liberal consensus for condemnation of grouse-shooters, I do not fully share this knee-jerk response; it does not give enough credit to the grouse. It should be remembered that most moors, like this one, are desolate, God-forsaken spots – windswept, sodden, featureless and freezing – and yet the grouse, single-handed, manages to lure half the ruling class into standing here for hours on end. This says much about their relative intelligence levels. Nor is the target just sitting there as defencelessly as the Hooray Henrys believe. For every grouse shot by the hunters, the coveys, in return, bag at least a brace of human, one with pneumonia, the other from hypothermia. As well as this, the grouse has probably killed off more of the landed gentry with trenchfoot than did the entire First World War. And still the upper classes don't twig! The red grouse are only declining in numbers today because, after centuries of successful stalking, they have so whittled down the aristocracy, and ensured their secret avian aim of a more classless society, that they are finally free to take up migration like normal birds.

The rest of the day is a blank in my mind; neither Bowes Moor nor Cotherstone Moor could manage a single feature between them. Apart from the brief and violent interruption of the A66, we saw no sign of a soul, alive or walking. As the afternoon and early evening wore on, the land rose and fell, and rose and fell, every time to reveal yet more moor, with each ridge an anti-climax, heralding a false dinner. Aus's morning bursts had become evening burn-outs, and we trudged – almost together – in silence, except for regular and over-eager offers to accommodate the other's need to rest. He had a worsening knee problem and I had a worsening boot problem – over and above our common body problems. We were in severe trouble; we looked and felt like the ones who get wrapped in silver foil at the end of the London marathon. But sadly, when breasting the hostel tape that night, we had merely reached the exact halfway point of the P.W. marathon, and here all you get wrapped in is black depression.

7 AS WEAK AS NEW BOOTS

I have many vivid memories of the Pennine Way, in both agony and ecstasy categories. The most abiding of these is the kitchen at Baldersdale Youth Hostel – or, more specifically, the planning of a meal therein. The kitchen was very large – in fact, it was too large for either of us to walk the length of in a single evening; the only part of either body still active was the stomach. We did not lack ingredients (the tin) nor the recipe ('make it boil'), but we were overwhelmed by the logistics. Our problem can be simply stated: utensils in zone A; cooker in zone B; saucepans in zone C; eating facilities in zone D; washing-up facilities in zone E. What is the minimum travelling distance necessary to prepare, cook, serve, eat, clear away, wash up and put away all the elements of an edible meal for two zombies? Answers on Y.H. membership cards only, please. (I understand this puzzle has already appeared in a Mensa Christmas Quiz.)

Absurd though it now seems, we were so exhausted that we did actually sit for some time not only discussing this matter, but even, with feeble, if not demented, giggles, drawing up an action-plan full of little arrows on a napkin; had we not later wiped the table with it, we might now both be holders of a NAAFI Ph.D. And then, painfully, slowly, and with much famine aforethought, we safely gathered in a little harvest of implements – an activity that took considerably more time than the cooking. But, at long last, dinner (loosely speaking) was ready. I can still remember us hobbling robotically to our seats, with our food cooling faster than we could walk, and sinking down in triumph

. . . and then asking each other to pass the salt . . . and then realising the nearest known salt cellar was 20 yards distant, with no possibility of anybody reaching it before daybreak.

The next day to break was a Friday, and the thirteenth day of the walk, and appropriately it brought steady, pouring rain. It also brought a rupture in North/South relationships.

There are several golden rules to a friendship. If one wishes to keep good friends, one should never share accommodation with them; nor work with them; nor go on holiday with them. Indeed, I now believe the only certain way to keep on good terms with close friends is to never see them at all. The crisis with Aus came when he refused point-blank to get up – ever again; from deep within many layers of the regulation-grey Y.H. blankets came an announcement that the time had arrived for him to realise a long-held ambition to die peacefully in his bed. Even the promise of a supplementary cornflake ration could not budge him. Between us for some days now (both days, in fact) there had been certain areas of conflict concerning the walk – in general, these were: starting walking, during walking, and stopping walking – and I had grown increasingly disappointed by his treating the trip as though it were some kind of leisure activity. When I tried to establish his bona fides for death, he simply claimed the trouble was an old war-wound – to some knee or other – and refused to wake up. For a while there seemed no way, short of a commercially-sponsored Pennine Way bed-pull, that he would carry on. But I knew that I had the majesty of the Warden on my side, so I decided to just wait, and passed the time by eating his supplementary cornflake ration. And then, as calculated, at the stroke of 10 the YHA Offences Against Hostelling Act came into force, which, since it carries the capital sentence of card destruction, was able to persuade him, at last, to rejoin the land of the partly-living.

Outside, with the scenery becoming pleasantly pastoral again, Friday the 13th brought the return of another,

82

deadlier, challenge: farmers. To many of them, walkers fall into a sub-species like boll weevil, greenfly and slugs, and in an ideal world would be got rid of with a can of something nasty. But this is not yet permitted, even under the Common Agricultural Policy, so instead, as I soon found out, land-owners put up electrified fences or raise bulls with a liking for human flesh. At least the electrified fences have a certain subtlety – they are usually erected with a professional knowledge of the distance above the ground of the average hiker's average private parts; one can either hurdle over them, and risk untold damage to future generations of little walkers, or limbo-dance underneath them, which, with a 35 lb rucksack, requires a sense of rhythm unknown outside the Caribbean. A bull, on the other hand, has no such subtlety. A bull is a bull is a bull. And a notice saying 'My bull can cross this field in under one minute. Can you?' poses a simple straightforward question, with no existential aspects that need concern one. The answer – no prizes given – is 'No'. (Only the previous day I had discovered, some feet in front of 40 tons of impending juggernaut, that I could not actually cross the A66 in under one minute. Even faced with imminent death, my legs could not break out of their concrete casing; transfixed in that road, amidst the smell of burning Euro-brake rubber, I had a sudden insight into the problems of daily life as a hedgehog – probably yet another species on the modern farmer's death list.) The best course of action, when faced with a bull, is, therefore, to distract it with a cow. If you do not have a cow with you, inform the bull, in a clear voice, of your rights, so that, in the event of your being gored to death, the animal cannot plead ignorance of the legal position. Do *not* kick it in the testicles, as this can make it very cross.

It was lunchtime, we had left Lunedale well behind, and my mind had been on cheese-and-onion crisps for a good hour, when suddenly we had a vision, a joint vision. In it,

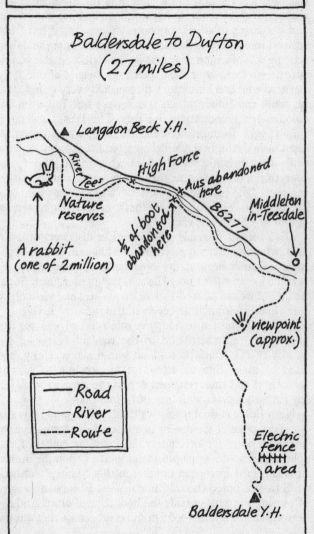

Baldersdale to Dufton
(27 miles)

▲ Langdon Beck Y.H.

River Tees

High Force

Aus abandoned here

Nature reserves

½ of boot abandoned here

B6277

Middleton-in-Teesdale

A rabbit
(one of 2 million)

— Road
~ River
---- Route

viewpoint
(approx.)

Electric
fence
⊢⊣⊢⊣⊢
area

▲ Baldersdale Y.H.

the sun burst forth, and a wondrous panorama stretched out below us. And lo, we had discovered Teesdale! Teesdale was a revelation to me, not only for its superb landscape, but also because it had employed a different painter and decorator to all the previous valleys, and I felt I had strayed into a foreign land. For mile after mile the colour scheme was of a man very heavily into white, and it was no surprise to learn later the explanatory legend of one Lord Barnard who had his estate whitewashed every year so that he could remember which farms were his. But even the colours were secondary to the Tees. The Tees is a wonderfully-rough, disgracefully-behaved river, whose waterfalls must have the highest decibel count in the country, and the walk along its banks was absolute exhilaration. And, to cap everything, the river runs through acre after acre of nature reserves, all containing flowers which elsewhere are becoming so depressingly rare that they will soon have to be grown in a Securicor van.

Discovery of Teesdale was rather like discovery of Smirnoff, whereby they say anything can happen. It did. In the midst of such beauty, my boot collapsed and Aus's leg became loose at the knee. His was the greater need. So, as neither of us had packed a spare cartilage, I had virtually to carry him (an ironic role-reversal, this) across the river (by footbridge, I hasten to add; the role-reversal was not *that* spectacular) and help him to the roadside verge of the nearby B6277. Once there, I sat him down carefully, and tried to make him as attractive as possible to passing motorists, and then returned across the river to work out my future progress with one and a half boots.

High Force is the biggest waterfall in England; it is also the most popular viewpoint in all Teesdale. I sat there for nearly an hour. Unfortunately, all I can remember of that spectacular scene is planning a campaign to halt the import of cheap East European boots into this country – at least until they adopted the traditional West European concept of putting the nails outside the boot instead of in. And the reason I stayed sitting for 55 minutes is because that was the time it took me to pack my right boot with the Northern edition of the Radio Times. From now on, I was walking on a wing and a prayer and a programmes listing.

It was a long, slow toil along the upper Tees to Langdon Beck Youth Hostel – so slow that I almost got on first-name terms with some of the several million rabbits, and so long that I even began to tire of beauty. The sun was not the only one to have a sinking feeling. I was the hapless inheritor of Aus's late start. Aus, however, was not – when I limped in too late for the hostel dinner, he was sitting happy and well-fed in a large armchair and waxing lyrical about the advantages of hitch-hiking the Pennine Way.

I had not the energy to make a proper meal, so I just licked one or two people's tin-openers and went to bed early.

I am not over-fond of dormitories. Before lights-out, they are full of unknown people with unknown standards of hygiene and disconcerting tastes in underwear; after lights-out, they are full of eccentric breathing patterns and unidentifiable body odours. There are often sleep-talkers, there can be sleep-walkers, there might well be sleep-psychopaths. It is not conducive to knitting up the ravell'd sleeve of care.

That particular night, the main threat to sleep came from three young lads suffering from what they insouciantly referred to as 'the Pennine Way lergie'; principal among its medical features, I gathered, was an unpredictable and uncontrollable urge to vomit with a violence that carried the previous day's food to a distance of about fifteen yards – as had indeed, they said, happened the previous night, causing the evacuation of an entire room (and, I suppose, most of a stomach). Although, fortunately, their prognosis was faulty, I spent several sleepless hours on red alert, waiting to be engulfed by a tidal wave of very *basse cuisine*. More unfortunately, however, old Ivan, in the bunk above me, really did have a weak bladder. Eight times in that one night he came down the creaking bed frame, putting a large Polish foot in my mouth, and falling heavily to the floor.

87

Each time, he would open several cupboard doors before successfully leaving the room, and then, after a brief interlude of suspense, the sounds of a pre-war plumbing system making contact with a flush toilet would reverberate distastefully through the wall. There would then follow the stumbling return. Ivan's most dramatic re-entry of the night came when he fell full-length over my rucksack and, in the pitch-dark, carefully and politely replaced it upside down, thus re-distributing its entire, decaying contents to all four corners of the dormitory. This produced widespread hysteria – in which I took no part.

Friday the 13th over, Aus and I made new plans. His knee now heavily strapped, we agreed to go each at his own pace. Unfortunately, I could still not keep up with him, and we did not meet again until after lunch, which he was carrying.

It was a day of mixed emotions. It began with the powerfully remote quality of the upper Tees, its scattered white farms and lonely landscape reminiscent of a crofting settlement on some distant Scottish island, and the boulder-strewn path along the river bank looked wild enough to have seen its share of Sherpas. Therefore, as I climbed up the slippery rock by the dramatic 200 foot cataract of Cauldron Snout, it came as a great shock to see suddenly a drab concrete dam and realise that here the mighty Tees springs, or, rather, squirts from the infamous Cow Green reservoir. An internationally-recognised site for rare alpine plants, it was for this land that, in a 1960s conservation *cause célèbre*, the powers-that-be took on the beauties-that-be, and as so often won, flooding the valley, and saying, no doubt, 'Let them grow water-lilies!' I have since seen photos of this valley taken in the 1940s by an earlier, luckier walker; given the vast scale of the vandalism that government bodies indulge in, the only surprise to me is that the private individuals who wreck railway carriages and urinate in telephone boxes do not automatically qualify for government grants. Regrettably, the battle for Cow Green was fought and lost in the early days

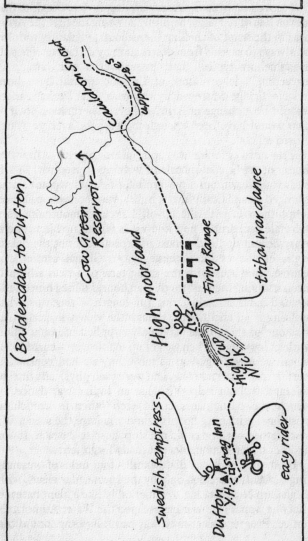

MAP 7: SECT.B

(Baldersdale to Dufton)

Cauldron Snout

upper Tees

Cow Green Reservoir

High moorland

Firing Range

tribal war dance

High Cup Nick

Swedish temptress

Dufton
Y.H. Stag Inn

easy rider

of the conservation movement, before David Bellamy was available to be drowned for good causes.

I moved on from the reservoir, deeply depressed, to find next a line of red flags, helpfully advising me that the Army was in the habit of shelling thereabouts, vigilantly training as always to save us from destruction by distant enemies. It is somehow typical that, just about a mile away, an exceedingly large chunk of England should have been systematically destroyed by our own side. Perhaps there should be a change of Army policy; a short sharp shell or two would have been enough to deter the average Water Board official.

The next emotion was total astonishment. After two hours of traditional moorland walking at around 1,900 ft the ground, without any warning, or AA viewpoint signs, plunged dramatically away into a vast horseshoe-shaped amphitheatre, with the far-off Lakeland mountains as a fairytale backdrop. I now know it as High Cup Nick, and it was without doubt the most unexpected, if not the finest, sight of the entire Pennine Way. 'Glacial erosion, of course,' said Aus with the smug tone of a man who had been studying the view for over an hour. I joined him on the ground, and stretched out full-length – *this* was what walking is all about. But, though the view was perfect, it was one of those clear days only supplied in conjunction with an icy wind. When we got up to move on – correction, when we *tried* to get up to move on, we had contracted permafrost of the marrow, and were each physically unable to stand without help. Visualise an Indian war dance, in which the participants circle each other in crouching positions, grimacing horribly, and you have the scene. We started to laugh, and could not stop, despite the pain. It was another of those moments not easily forgotten.

From then on it was all downhill – four miles of unremitting descent, redeemed only by the spectacular views, with High Cup Nick looking so remarkably like a giant bathtub that one wonders how it has escaped the Water Authority's notice. Progress, as always, was painfully slow, but as the fields and hedgerows came into clearer focus the surroundings grew more and more idyllic; this would have been the ideal moment to sonnetise about the English pastoral scene, and to lyricise about the sheep and their shepherd, but unfortunately I cannot think of a rhyme for the three-wheeler motorised BMX that the herdsman was gunning across the meadows in hot pursuit of his flock.

The other jarring experience of the afternoon was the stony track, and by the time we had reached the sunlit village green of Dufton, Aus's cartilage was ready for the pickling bottle. His knee would have gone to the top of any hospital waiting-list, and it was clear that, this time, he really was at journey's end. It was sad, for we both knew that when, in later years, his children asked, 'And what did *you* do during the Great Walk, daddy?' he would only have a very sick note to show them. But although Aus was disappointed and upset to throw in the towel and take an early bath, I felt more ambivalent. I had lost an occasional companion and a left knee I knew well, but I had probably saved a friendship. On the other hand, I did not relish the prospect of being alone once more, in, as it were, mobile solitary confinement.

Apart from the imminent threat of amputation, Dufton was a perfect end to any day: a lovely village, a village shop, a village green, even a village pub, where we soon went for a more pleasant jarring experience. The pub is called the Stag Inn, and I doubt there has yet entered a weary hosteller who has resisted the joke about 'Staggering In.' Except possibly for Ingrid.

The loneliness of the long-distance runner is well-known, but the fantasies of the long-distance walker are an aspect of outdoor activity rarely made public. The Ramblers' Association prefers to concentrate on muscle and sweat and map references, but if the truth about the real thoughts of ramblers, alone for hours in deep heather, were to be made known, then the R.A. could double its membership tomorrow, even if it were with the entire readership of *Penthouse* magazine; in the isolation of the

91

hills, there is only so much flora and fauna that a man – even the most ardent naturalist – can think about. The farmers understand this best, and one of the first sights above Edale on Day One was of sheep with the letters NO stamped in purple on their rumps, though whether this was to deter the more desperate hiker or the more literate ram, was never altogether clear. It was therefore disconcerting to see fantasy made flesh in the Stag Inn.

A single woman is rare on the Pennine Way. A beautiful, single, Swedish woman is even rarer. A beautiful, single, Swedish woman who is interested in company is probably unique. I offered to buy her a crate of lager.

I was not looking over-smart, unless mildew was, unbeknownst to me, now being marketed as chic, but we got on extremely well. She had not only conquered that last bastion of a foreign language, the humour, but her command of English was also rather better than anybody else's I had met en route. In a very short time, we were culturally exchanging with great zest. Her presence was particularly refreshing as it was some days since I had heard a Swedish view of the world.

The pleasure of her company was heightened because the occupational hazard of the P.W. route is the P.W. bore. Whenever two or three walkers are gathered together in the name of the Pennine Way, the conversation will always turn, at once, to confusing tracks, misleading signposts, comparative depths of alternative bogs, illicit short-cuts, worst stretches, best stretches, good hostels, bad hostels, injuries, blisters, pus problems, time taken, time lost, time to be allowed, etcetera, etcetera, etcetera; each day, the post-mortems (not in the literal sense, unless it was a very bad day) are repetitive, obsessive, inexhaustible, and proof that travel deadens the mind. Only occasionally does one not have to listen to all these wearisome details – and that is because one is recounting them oneself. No one is immune. The walk and all its minutiae so permeated every waking – and sleeping – hour that, as the miles had piled up, I found great pleasure in being an ever better-qualified bore, and

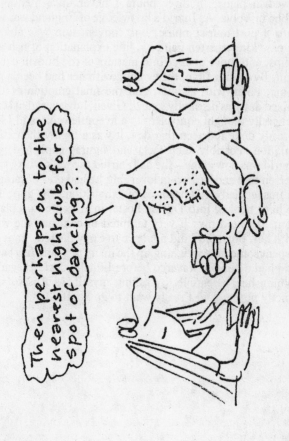

had come to look upon any chance to exchange mind-boggling P.W. trivia as just about the most satisfying moment of the day.

For once, however, it was back to good old-fashioned boy meets girl stuff, but on a very sophisticated Anglo-Swedish plane: in three hours I never once mentioned Abba or Volvo. As Ingrid's knowledge of England was well into a post-tourist phase, our conversation was able to bypass kindergarten gambits, like explanation of fish and chips, and move at once into matters of the human condition. By closing time, the evening with her had been a real tonic, taken with alcohol, and the final emotion of that mixed day was distinctly sexual. Given, however, that sex is generally thought equivalent to a five mile walk, and I had already done fourteen that day, it was a highly theoretical emotion. Possibly such facts and figures explained why Ingrid was now alone – she had started the walk with a two-person tent and a camp-in lover, but he had now decamped in unspecified circumstances of exhaustion. She appeared to have booked into Dufton hostel in search of a replacement. I found myself very tempted to continue the walk with her, provided I did not have to carry the tent. Indeed, I spent some time weighing up the many pros and few cons, and had definitely wavered before I finally decided against joining her, essentially by asking myself, as Aus so succinctly put it, 'Did I really want to go South?'

8 WEAR AND TEAR AND TYNE

It was 6 a.m. when I crept on tiptoe, alone and the first, out of Dufton Youth Hostel the next morning. Day Fifteen was not going to be easy. From Dufton to Alston there are twenty miles to be walked and four mountains to be climbed, all in the one day. Each peak is over 2,500 ft and that includes the highest top of the entire journey, 2,930 ft Cross Fell.

The day was already warm and very still. Only the sun and the keener flies were up – or so I thought. I had climbed steadily up through the fields to 1,500 ft, and was already sweating when I first saw him. Above me, at over 2,000 ft, was a figure. It ran forward five yards, it ran backward five yards; forward, backward, forward, backward. It got no nearer; it got no farther; it did nothing else. As I climbed inexorably closer, I tried to construct a reasonable explanation, but always came back to my limited knowledge of mad axe-men. He was still running, repetitively, maniacally, to and fro, and I was still pondering the correct conversational openings to use with deranged psychopaths, when we came face to face, with 100 square miles of Cumbria spread below us.

'Hallo,' he said. 'They're late!' (Some form of delusionary illness, I decided.)

'Yes . . . ' I replied – in a tone aimed at that delicate balance of being both understanding yet unpatronising in a single word at the same time.

'You had me worried. I thought you were one of them!' (With strong paranoiac elements, I further noted.)

'No! Oh no! No, no!' I had felt here that lashings of firm

reassurance were clearly required. 'No, no!' At this point, one of my own inner voices advised me to try and build a bond. 'One of what? I enquired.

'The relay team. Chris Brasher's lot.'

It is deflating, when one has 164 blood-stained, sweat-spattered miles stowed beneath an increasingly loose belt, to be accused of slowness by fitness freaks running the complete distance in less than 30 hours.

There are, in fact, various records. Somewhere that June a woman was running it in under five days. A man has since run it under three days. And the Holmfirth Harriers have completed it in 1 day 5 hours 46 minutes 17 seconds. Personally, I identified rather more with the two middle-aged couples I met in Lothersdale who had taken six years – so far. (Each pair owns a Dormobile, and whenever a free, sunny weekend occurs they park them a few miles apart and walk a section, exchanging car keys in mid-route.) As I grow older, I feel strongly that slow is beautiful. There is, however, a new generation of walkers afoot, for whom the principal pleasure offered by the countryside is to establish the shortest possible time required to pass through it. More and more walkers boast of the distance covered, not the sights seen, and any aesthetic features fall into the category of potential obstacles. It would seem provocative rhetoric to say that even nature is an unwelcome distraction to them, had I not actually seen Pennine Way walkers striding purposefully by with Walkmen clamped firmly to their ears, their expressions glazed, and the music finely tuned, no doubt, to drown out any obtrusive bird-song. (Presumably it is these walkers of the future who, at Dufton Hostel, – one of the most relaxing and sympathetic of rural hostels – regularly write in the Suggestions Book to complain at the absence of video games. When I first read that, I felt a touch of the old fogeys coming on, and had to be restrained from writing underneath that cold showers at dawn be made compulsory.)

After a pleasant little man-to-man chat with the relay runner, about such matters as my bronze medal for the

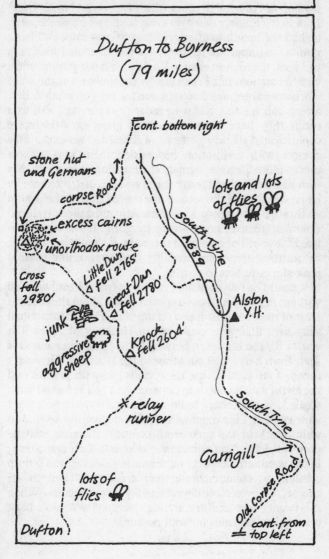

MAP 8: SECT. A

Dufton to Byrness
(79 miles)

Cont. bottom right

stone hut
and Germans

corpse Road

excess cairns

unorthodox route

lots and lots
of flies

South Tyne

A689

Little Dun
fell 2765'

Cross
fell
2980'

Great Dun
fell 2780'

Alston
Y.H.

junk

Knock
fell 2604'

aggressive
sheep

South Tyne

relay
runner

Garrigill

lots of
flies

Old Corpse Road

Dufton

cont. from
top left

under-11s long jump, I left him still waiting, his relay team clearly running late, and continued on up to tick off the summit of Knock Fell, after which I set about No. 2, Great Dun Fell. (Embarrassingly, when he did race past me, only he had the breath to offer greetings.) Great Dun Fell has a number of important features, like the watershed spawning the Tees, the highest road in England, a radar station, and a weather station, but I shall always remember it as the place where two sheep tried to mug me for my jam sandwiches. Sheep cohabit this hill with radar-type persons, and as a result they have been weaned off grass onto the more sophisticated dietary patterns of discarded tin-cans. This contact with civilisation has misled them into a most unsheeplike lifestyle, namely the hustling of humans. My own pair worked as a team: the first sheep distracted me by being cute, while the second one moved in from behind to go through my rucksack pockets. Any resistance produced a very aggressive, no-nonsense nuzzling. If Darwin calculated the speed of evolution correctly, it should not be long before these sheep are breeding man, and selling tasteful pink-skin artefacts to visiting flocks.

It would be remiss of me to move on from Great Dun Fell without first having a good abusive moan about the hideous mass of junk metal dumped on top of it. The old music-hall song says that 'you could see to Hackney Marshes if it wasn't for the houses in between'; the hiker's version says that, from here, 'you could see to the Irish Sea if it wasn't for the four giant masts, the various tacky tin prefabs and the awful squalid sheds in between.' As golf is a good walk spoiled, so a Ministry building seems always to be a good view ruined. This mountain-top is a depressing section to walk. Back in the nineteenth century, the rich and the powerful put up monuments to celebrate their egos; now, in the twentieth century, public authorities seem to put up eyesores to commemorate their crassness. There is, of course, one even more depressing aspect to progress. When the twenty-first century arrives, we may well look back upon this monstrous lot with nostalgia.

After mountain No 3, Little Dun Fell, it was on and up to the biggest and best, Cross Fell. The giant of the Pennine Way, this is where all the winds meet, where every view is recommended, and where the very grandest rivers begin.

It is also where the thickest mist lives, so the above information is courtesy of a textbook. Kinder Downfall, Penyghent, Great Shunner Fell, and now Cross Fell, all had been one great mystery (no pun intended) tour. From the viewpoint of views, I would have done better to take my exercise at home on a walking machine placed within sight of the garden. Among the many unexpected walkers of the Pennine Way has been a blind man; in case he found the experience frustrating, I would like to reassure him that a lot of the time he missed absolutely nothing.

For once, even the cairn system broke down. (Cairns are the safeguard whereby walkers are saved from straying off the crooked and narrow; it is not done, *pace* RSPCA, by placing small dogs at regular intervals for hundreds of miles, but by building up piles of loose stones along the route.) In my earliest, most ignorant, phase, I had been baffled by these heaps. At first I had vaguely assumed they must be part of some worthy scheme to Keep Upland Britain Tidy; but, as the miles passed, I abandoned that idea in favour of the more worrying theory that they were burial sites for The Unknown Walker – suggesting a toll not far short of Passchendaele. Their true purpose was then explained to me. I was most impressed – principally because I understood it to mean that walkers carried up their own stones from home. I was then afflicted by guilt for days.

The problem with Cross Fell was the sheer abundance of stones. There were cairns everywhere. The summit is a huge, rock-strewn plateau, and I spent a good hour on a circular cairn tour. Quite clearly, walkers with nothing to do – and there is very little to do on Cross Fell in thick mist – pass their time by building vast piles of stones just for the hell of it. The final straw came when I approached one hazy cairn only to see it get up and walk away. It was a sheep.

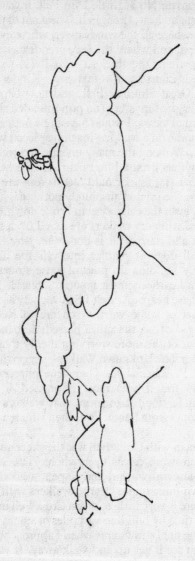

Perhaps it was taking revenge for the jam sandwiches.

By sheer fluke, I found a small stone shelter. Inside it was one-quarter full of walkers, three-quarters full of empty beer cans. There were two taciturn Germans and an Australian, who said they had been waiting for the view for three days. I was about to laugh, but became uncertain when I noticed they all had about three days' stubble on their chins. I joined them where they sat, crouched low in the shelter, unsmiling and cold, alternately belching and crushing cans. The Germans were grim, hard men, with that intimidating look of seasoned travelling bums taking time out from being mercenaries. Conversation was slow.

After a short while I decided to try and leave, and set off on the first of several reverse circular tours of the cairns. At one point, an Air/Sea Rescue helicopter flew low overhead. I was unsure whether this was encouraging or worrying. All my books referred to the great difficulty of finding the correct route off the summit in mist, and went, I thought, into unnecessary archaeological detail about the numerous hidden mine-shafts nearby. Only by much trial and terror did I find the track down. It was yet another of those dreadful stony descents, but this was the Daddy of them all, seven miles long and called 'the corpse road', though whether it carried corpses or turned people into them was not made clear.

It was 9 p.m. when I crept flat-footed, alone and the last, towards Alston Youth Hostel, perfectly placed on the banks of the South Tyne. I had bad memories of Alston, lovely market town though it is. On my first visit here, as a teenager, I had found myself so short of money that my parents had to intercede with the IMF to get me home. On my second visit, as an adult, I had arrived in a tropical downpour; my windscreen wipers packed up, and the repair had cost slightly more than the car to which they were attached. This was my third visit, strictly economy class. Unfortunately, I had not realised that Alston Youth Hostel closed on Sundays. When I left town the next morning I was twenty pounds lighter and walking with new slim-line pockets.

I stayed in a pub, which was full of happy people who all knew each other. This is the worst type of loneliness. So I went out to a restaurant, which was full of more happy people who all knew each other. And I felt even lonelier. So I retired very early upstairs to my bedroom, which was full of the sound of happy people downstairs – until very late. I have had better ends to better days.

The reward for Cross Fell was a day's valley-walking to Hadrian's Wall. The weather was fine, the scenery was lovely, and my companion for the day was the beautiful and shapely South Tyne. (The Tyne, like the Tees, has a legendary industrial ring to us Southerners, and it comes as a great surprise to find it is not filled with coal dust.) Yet, all in all, it was a thoroughly disagreeable day. Once off the spine of England, the Pennine Way seemed to lose any interest in being a serious, conscientious walk – faced with the A689 also going North along the valley, it suffered one of its periodic fits of road-shyness, and tacked desperately from side to side, making as much rational progress as a small boy trying to walk without stepping on the cracks between paving-stones. But one could at least follow paving-stones – the patchwork of fields was more baffling than a featureless tract of moorland, and it needed a compass with psychic powers to divine the right of way. Oddly though, it was this very reaction of impatience which suddenly made me realise for the first time that I now believed – failing Acts of God or the devil – I really might just make it through to the very end; if I had been a bookie, I would have thought 5–4 on to be very fair odds.

The other unpleasant aspect of this idyllically warm lowland day was the complete absence of any rain or cold or wind. In their place was a capacity attendance of flies. We humans listen to weather forecasts to plan our days; I think flies listen to human forecasts to plan theirs. No sooner had my perspiration set foot outside my armpits than they turned up like an unwanted escort agency. It is hard to imagine a globule of sweat having the appeal of Chanel No. 5,

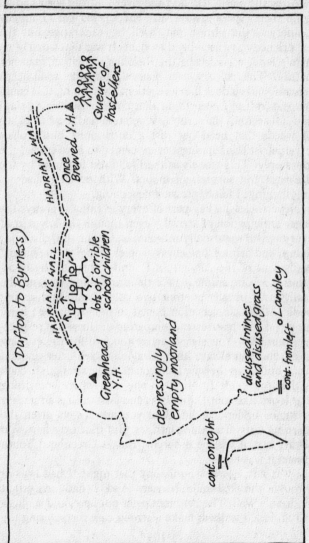

MAP 8: SECT. B

(Dufton to Byrness)

Queue of hostellers

Once Brewed Y.H.

HADRIAN'S WALL

lots of 'orrible school children

HADRIAN'S WALL

Greenhead Y.H.

depressingly empty moorland

cont. o'night

disused mines and disused grass

o Lambley

cont. from left

but I was quite evidently the sexiest beast along the South Tyne that day.

After the warm day and the river and the road had all gone their separate ways, the last lap led past Lambley Colliery – the phrase may well be alliterative but the experience was miserably dissonant. It was that worst of no man's land, a landscape that belongs to neither man nor nature. The colliery was disused, but the spoil-heaps remain, and so does the dereliction. Everything that could rot was rotting, everything that could rust was rusting, and, all around, the scrubby vegetation had the sick pallor of weeds that need not just a nutritionist but a plant psychiatrist. Unhappiness even seemed to have turned the grass grey. This scene was then followed for miles by the dreariest and soggiest of moors. With evening shadows lengthening, I felt depression deepening.

Nevertheless, a key part of every evening is always the eager anticipation of arrival – even though the key part of every arrival was usually anti-climax. Out on the fells, cold, damp, and aching, one always comes to expect the hikers' equivalent of the Algonquin Round Table, to the background accompaniment of a thousand guitars – and the reality was usually another two cold, damp and aching bodies, their conversation honed to monosyllables, lying prone on bare mattresses, comparing the merits of respective liniments. You always arrive too late for the evening meal, and you always limp off alone to self-cater under a bleak bulb, and the only food you have the strength to cook is that inevitable full-meal-in-one-can, where something that looks like soup, chipolatas and custard has an uneasy existence under one lid. And you are always given the morning duty of cleaning latrines. But the next night, you always say, it will be different. But at Greenhead Youth Hostel it was not.

I was not, however, unhappy that night. I had broken through the 200 mile barrier. And I had arrived at Hadrian's Wall. The Pennines peter out here, and geologically-minded walkers make a strong case for petering the

104

walk out here as well. Personally, I have always felt there was a strong case for stopping the walk somewhere near Kinder Scout, but then I am more of a geriatrically-minded walker. I decided to treat myself to an easy day, and to walk just the seven miles eastward along the Wall to the next hostel.

I have a terrible guilty confession to make about Hadrian's Wall. I was not all that impressed. I agree that as an ancient Scot it might have made me think twice about visiting relatives in England, but it did not seem as high as its hype. Somehow, ever since childhood history lessons, I had imagined a structure so vertiginous that even King Kong would have needed grappling irons; in fact, I have seen higher garden walls in Surbiton. (Where, admittedly, the bourgeoisie are currently in greater danger from burglars than the Romans ever were. It is my opinion that the true test of a good wall is how well you can see it from the moon, and Hadrian's is apparently not even visible with bifocals. As it has been vandalised from its original height of fifteen feet down to its present one of little more than six, it is evident that the real building achievement in Northumberland is now to be found in massively-elaborate local rock-gardens. I also have serious geo-military and strategic reservations. Given that much of the wall is on the top of sheer cliffs anyway, I would have thought all that Mr Hadrian needed was a fast-moving regimental psychopathum with an urn or two of boiling woad.

Possibly my viewpoint was clouded – as was the icy-cold, wet and windy day – by a surfeit of schoolchildren. The path rose and fell like a Big Dipper, and slithering up and down every slope were riotous crocodiles of unregimented kiddy-winkies. Struggling along in stiletto heels and flipflops, effing and blinding in the usual way of twelve and thirteen-year-olds, and fighting for possession of one or two communal plastic macs, their exposure to archaeological miracles did not seem to be realising its educational potential. Consequently, any leap of my more poetic imagination was aborted at take-off.

105

I retain a deep scepticism of school trips. I can still vividly remember my own grand tour of Venice and Florence at the age of fourteen, when my main response to the wonders of the Renaissance was to spend most of each day in back-street cafés gambling my allowance of funny money on games of table football with young Italianate Arfur Daleys; the architectural climax of the trip, a visit to the massive cathedral dome in Florence, remains principally memorable for a Newtonian experiment in which four of us tried to establish whether, if released simultaneously, it would be a five-lira piece or a gob of spit that arrived on the ground first. So, as I made my way along through hordes more numerous and barbaric than the original legionaries – and generally doing more damage to Hadrian's handiwork than two and a half centuries of irate proto-Scots – I did wonder at the trip's worth, and indeed its exact purpose. My great hope was that it might be a Classics party and that the absence of any teachers indicated a noble attempt to re-enact the Oedipus practice of small children being abandoned to die on hostile mountainsides. Given that, at Edale, school parties had cost me a night's sleep, and at Stainforth, cost me a night's bed, and now on Hadrian's Wall, a day's peace, I felt this traditional approach to the under-16s should be more widely incorporated into the 1944 Education Act.

It was a unique experience to arrive at a Youth Hostel and find it closed because I was too early. I was not, however, unique in arriving too early, because the wind and the rain had made many turn their back to the Wall, and there was a queue that would not have disgraced a No. 11 bus. Indeed, a lot of the waiting walkers looked more familiar with a bus than a hostel, for this, once again, was tourist territory, and there were whole families looking shiny, and crackling noisily whenever they tried to breathe in their new anoraks.

Families on hostelling holidays seem an oddly archaic breed. They tend to talk and cook and eat in hermetically-sealed units; artificially cheerful and with a Blue Peter politeness, even to each other, they look as if their presence were due to a Tardis with the wrong landing co-ordinates. For me, their happy hostelling has a clearly legible subtext: father is suffering from delusions of nostalgia. All too often, one senses a family dragged along to relive a father's 30-year-old memories of traditional lumberjack values. Having hostelled when A roads were B roads, and motorways were still fields, he wants the childhood of the father revisited on the son, and to raise the second generation with a shared belief in bunk beds and unconditioned air. But, deep down, the son would rather the bright lights and lead pollution, the daughter thinks she has just become busted enough to go topless in Ibiza, and the mother would prefer waitress service. No one, of course, says so. Even father's spiritual successors, the hairy, hearty back-packers, are the far side of a generation gap.

Maladjusted parents were not the only distinctive feature of Once Brewed Youth Hostel. I spent the night in a dormitory filled with a party of Cambridge undergraduates whose every step was sponsored for the physically disabled, a minority group in which I was now entitled to life membership. Before the night was over I felt entitled to sponsorship for sharing a dormitory with Cambridge undergraduates. Some people talk in their sleep, but gilded youth talk in other people's sleep; they also spend the night pillow-fighting and making rude noises, and being very witty with buckets of water. I have a lot of sympathy with the less fortunate members of society, and I think it is about time the physically disabled tried to do something to help Cambridge undergraduates – surely theirs is not an affliction totally without cure?

The next day brought more wind, more rain, and more Wall, but also a panorama utterly compelling in its stark grandeur. For the first time, the clouds allowed a Roman's eye view; had the second century A.D. not been The Age of Blood and Guts, every centurion here would have laid down his axe and become a landscape artist, so tremendous are the views from coast to coast. But there is a great

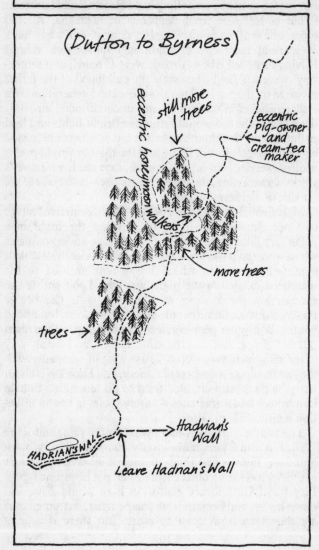

MAP 8: SECT. C

(Dufton to Byrness)

still more trees

eccentric honeymoon walkers

eccentric pig-owner and cream-tea maker

more trees

trees →

HADRIAN'S WALL

Hadrian's Wall

Leave Hadrian's Wall

change, alas, in the views to the North. Today, Hadrian's Wall looks as though it were built to keep out the regiments of pine that are marching remorselessly across the horizon like an arboreal master race. Descending steeply from the Wall, the route follows an old drovers' road across the moors and into the Border Forest, the largest man-made forest in Britain.

Forestry Commission plantations are to proper countryside what inflatable rubber dolls are to sex – a sad perverted parody of the real thing. The very contours of the land itself are submerged, with every feature buried in a uniform green blur. One trudges through these plantations for ever; no sound enters, no light enters, no life appears. It has the deathliness of a walk round a padded cell, and the aesthetics of a city tour by underground. Even the trees looked terminally ill with depression; economic forestry has been compared to battery farming and it is an apt description. It is also said that pine trees suffer excessively from acid rain; it is my view that they are drinking it to commit suicide. Ironically, it is the 'ecologically-concerned citizen' that so often belongs to the trendy world of pine-buyers who provide the economic stimulus to ravage the very ecology they campaign to protect. (The ultimate outrage occurs some miles off the route near Kielder Dam. There, the Forestry Commission actually *charges* 50 pence for a scenic drive through the forest. Given the vast public funds used to ruin the countryside with conifers, it does seem rather unreasonable to then charge the taxpayer to view the damage done with his own money. Surely they should pay us? If only as a penance.)

There were just two moments of light relief in all that grim, dark day. At one point, I emerged – God knows where! – upon a clearing and a small road – and a parked camper van. And a mug of waiting tea. It was offered to me by a cheerful man in his fifties, who explained he was the back-up team and support system – a sort of motorised Sherpa – for an expedition moving South, to Edale. This consisted of his wife, his grown-up daughter and his son-in-law, two of whom were on their honeymoon, and all of whom, in his opinion, were quite mad. He had been exempted from conscription himself, he said, by putting in a competitive tender for the catering services and, as a result, he had Northumberland's largest collection of mobile baked beans. But the group were very poor navigators, he thought, and as they might be in the forest for some weeks yet, he was prepared to victual any passing walker in need. I had a second mug of tea. And then I set off into the maw of the forest again. I met the bizarre ménage à trois about a mile further on, in a torrential downpour. They were easily identifiable, as the mother-in-law had on a mac, a plastic hood and thigh-length boots. They were all remarkably happy and cheerful, particularly the two women who were having all their luggage carried for them in large bags by the man. They asked about the Dormobile and if I had had a cup of tea. When, in turn, I tried to gently probe them, and their reason for this unorthodox form of honeymoon, the daughter simply said it got her mother out of the house, which seemed to me a somewhat drastic solution given that a visit to the pub would have achieved the same effect. And then they all set off again through the mud.

The second oddity of the day came mid-afternoon at a farmhouse. For miles past, at every nook and spinney, there had been scribbled and painted notices to the effect that it served homemade teas. A farmhouse tea! Clotted cream, perhaps! Maybe a log fire! It was a long, cold climb to the farm and a rising wind was doing a fair imitation of a hurricane when I knocked on the kitchen door. It was still rising when, after several knocks, I was shown through . . . into the farmyard, on the top of the hill, where I shivered hungrily on a bench. Ten minutes and several pullovers later, an old lady appeared with a metal tray, on which stood two rockcakes and an iced drink. In the mounting tempest I secured the tray to the table with a brick and tried to sit upwind of the repast; only the lead content of the rockcakes was preventing lift-off. My mistake was to pick

110

up the drink can. Immediately, the tray, the plate, the glass, and the alleged cakes hurtled the full length of the farmyard. I staggered after them. At that precise moment, the largest pig in the world burst through a sty door. It had a snout start. 'Shoo!' I cried. 'Shoo!'

Amazing speed, pigs. It cost me £1.20 to feed that animal.

For two whole days the rain had not ceased, except to allow the wind to have a go. There is rain, heavy rain, torrential rain, and walkers' rain; walkers' rain specialises in penetrating all materials guaranteed waterproof. Consequently, arrival at Bellingham Youth Hostel, a large wooden hut near the North Tyne, was like arrival at a Chinese laundry. Centre-stage was an old stove, surrounded by what appeared to be the contents of a shipwreck. Surveying the scene was a handful of nudist hostellers, standing in thick steam, and humidly disputing the territorial rights of each other's lingerie. Being a seasoned traveller, I at once opened negotiations for a piece of real estate with a view of the fire, and prepared to lay my Y-fronts on the line. I too had not so much as a dry handkerchief to wear. But – and this is probably of more widespread public concern – as I poured (a carefully-chosen word) my unworldly belongings into the daylight, I became embarrassingly aware that, even when dry, I was no longer in possession of a single garment acceptable to the most broadminded of Oxfam shops. And this raises a central issue of long-distance walking about which I am often sent stamped addressed envelopes in confidence: hygiene.

The greatest personal challenge a Pennine Way walker can face is hygiene. On the walk, cleanliness is not so much next to Godliness as next to miraculous. I am not speaking here of bodily ablutions – thanks to the cold-shower ethos, the under-arm quality control is first-class – but of clothing decay. The range of social events to which, after 225 miles, I could now be invited, was probably limited to celebration of the Vagrancy Act at Bellingham Police Station. The problem is that by arriving late every night, leaving early every morning, and being in a state of suspended animation in between, one is left no chance to experiment with the latest washing powders. The days of ramblers with a retinue of washerwomen are long gone. The hapless long-distance walker has just two choices: he can either carry a minimum of 20 spare pairs of socks, vests, underpants and shirts, or a washing machine. Or ask for a Red Cross emergency airlift of clothes parcels. I hope this advice is of some use.

This is probably the appropriate moment to also touch, delicately, on the single aspect of walking most responsible for deterring several million walkers every year: lack of toilet facilities. A week may be a long time in politics, but twelve hours is an eternity in the average digestive system. What is to be done? For the richer rambler – and indeed the four-course packed-lunch man – there is now a wheeled chemical latrines facility, with matching mini-marquee, on the market, but not all walkers find this practical. The alternative, non-chemical, solutions are not really a subject suitable for a family paperback, and therefore the best advice is to contact the YHA. This year they are bringing out an illustrated leaflet, Gippy Tummy on Moorland, which deals with all the dietary, social and ecological facets of being caught short; additionally, the Country Land-owners Association publish a small pamphlet called Wilderness Tracts versus Urinary Tracts, which explains the legal position, and the rights of gamekeepers in this matter.

All that I can remember of the following day, Day Nineteen seems remarkably similar to Day Eighteen. It rained a lot; there was a lot of boggy moorland, for which I am now bereft of adjectives; and there were a lot of pine trees, for which I now feel deficient in abuse. I talked to no one; I updated the edition of the Radio Times now forming 75 per cent of my right boot; and I walked a further sixteen miles.

This brought me to Byrness, which, I suspect, is North-umberland dialect for 'the place of much girding of loins.' A little forestry village, it is the launching pad for the final

113

MAP 8: SECT. D

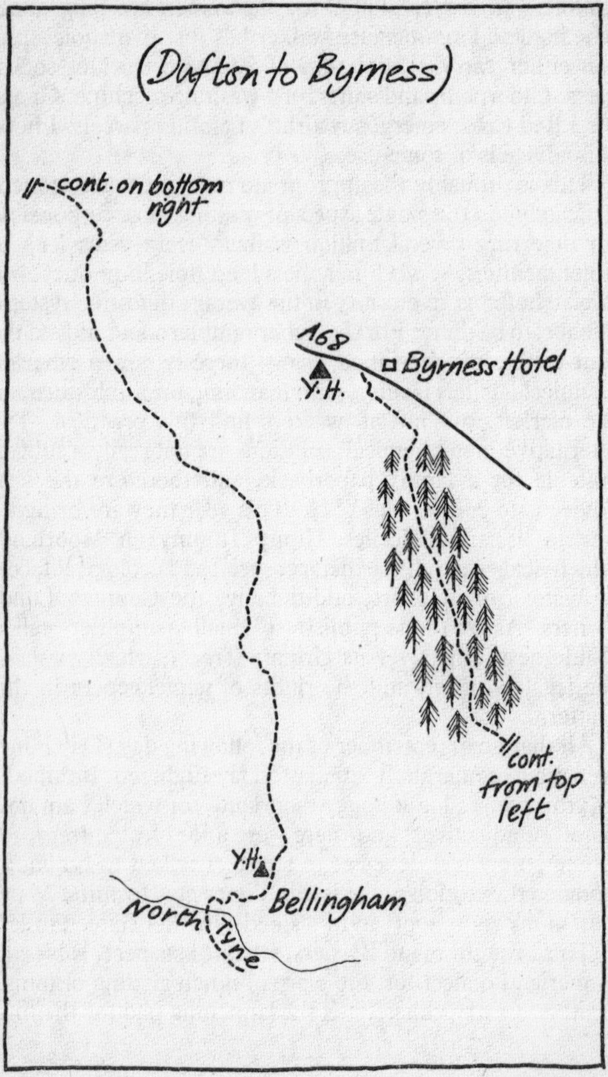

(Dufton to Byrness)

← cont. on bottom right

168
Y.H.

☐ Byrness Hotel

‖ cont. from top left

Y.H.
Bellingham

North Tyne

day, the longest, hardest, wildest day of all, along the top of the Cheviots. Here in the tiny hostel – two converted terrace cottages – a backlog of hikers often forms, like Everest mountaineers waiting at Base Camp for favourable weather and body conditions.

The condemned man likes to eat a hearty meal and I did just that at nearby Byrness Hotel. Indeed, it was a whole evening of forbidden delights. I saw television for the first time in nearly three weeks, which is possibly a national abstinence record; I talked to normal human beings with cars, who gave me information about the outside world – to my astonishment I discovered that Wimbledon and I had passed like tennis balls in the night; and I heard the rare sound of laughter, some of it, I believe, my own. At closing time, I walked the half-mile back to my mattress feeling well-cheered. It had not exactly been wine, women and song, but at least, for once, it had been beer, TV and chat.

9 SHOULDER TO THE GRITSTONE

It was D-Day, Day Twenty. The time 5.30 a.m. The place: Byrness Youth Hostel. The destination: Scotland – and journey's end, 29 gruelling miles away.

I was not alone. Half a dozen shadowy figures were bent double in the half-light around the bunk beds. I was with a small band of determined men who had assembled a larger collection of Elastoplast, crepe bandages, cotton wool, ankle supports, and embrocation than the free world of rambling had ever seen before. After 241 miles, each one of us was now highly trained, and could strap, splint, plaster, poultice and surgically dress himself in less than an hour. Our bodies ready, we tried to boost the morale of our kit. Rucksacks were checked for mice, socks were checked for daylight, oranges were checked for vitamins. For this final assault even the boots needed to be mentally prepared. Then, each compass was given its final set of instructions, and all of us were off, and on our way. The others were large, wild, hairy, beer-swilling, swearing Geordies – they were the sort of men's men who would have conquered the West, whereas I was more the sort of man who would have arrived a wee while later on, and opened a nice little haberdasher's shop. We set off at a scorching pace. It was, I think, as we crossed the village green just outside the hostel that I lost sight of them.

The dramatic ridge walk along the Cheviots regularly rises above 2,000 ft like a giant rollercoaster, and was yet another section constantly described by passing Jeremiads as the worst. This time, they were probably right. It was high, remote, endless, and with no escape route; at two

points, temporary shelters have been erected by walkers and in one of them a graffito reads 'Even Kilroy was not here.' Yet, for all the slog and bog, much of it was a wonderful walk. The scale of the scenery was the grandest yet, the density of population the smallest yet, and as I bestrode the mountains I was almost taken with an urge to yodel. The weather was a powerful mix of sun and storms, and the light on the surrounding mountains was constantly, dramatically changing (as indeed I was, in and out of my waterproofs). Somehow, though, up so high, I almost felt a participant in the weather, and really enjoyed watching the sheer theatre of the stormclouds racing from the horizon towards me, apparently with express instructions to deliver their goods personally.

The end result was a day of quite magnificent views – which was fortunate, for the walker who strays here in mist pays heavily. He is likely to be shot. This is not a Ramblers' Association penalty for sloppy walking, just the British Army on target practice once again. On these heights it is not the deer who stalk the land, but the MoD. I met one bemused walker who had stumbled into a CS gas attack; presumably, since the Falklands, crowd control of sheep is a high military priority. Dire notices warn humans of the edge of the firing range; one just hopes the bullets have been told where to stop. For mile after mile along the border the red flags fly; it did cross my mind that, being a far-flung outpost, nobody has yet informed it of the 1707 Act of Union, and our boys are still waiting for the Scots to attack.

The other outpost, Chew Green, is Roman. They, however, have definitely gone home, driven out, it would seem, by a well-organised army of archaeologists, and leaving behind them the most complicated and remarkable set of earthworks in the Roman Empire. (I speak, of course, not from research but plagiarism.) A more inaccessible and inhospitable spot for the excessive building of ramparts is hard to conceive. This extremely remote site has many mysteries, of which the most baffling is how the

118

Romans ever found their way up here at all without an Ordnance Survey map.

Indeed, how anyone managed any of the Pennine Way in pre-Wainwright days is a mystery. Wainwright is the Samuel Pepys of fell-walking, his eccentric 1967 guide still an unlikely best-seller – hand-written, pencil-sketched and reading perversely from back to front, it records every yard and every squelch. Approaching walkers can be seen from miles away clutching his work like Maoists stapled to the Little Red Book; with Wainwright, it is more reliable to read the scenery than look at it. But for him, I would have fallen at the first stile.

Indeed, although written in the days of pounds, shillings and pence, the work has worn rather better than the walk. Wainwright was describing pastures new and moorland rarely trespassed against. But what was then a foible of eccentrics, is now a business worth billions, because walking has come of age for all ages. Since leisure has been made more compulsory, B & B more available and the signpost industry more developed, the mass desire to escape the masses has so wrecked parts of the P.W. that they are now the width of a passable, though impassable, dual carriageway. And, ominously, the march of history is starting to trample over familiar ground – in the last century, it was the major routes of trade that were churned into vast seas of mud; today it is the trunk routes of walking which suffer that fate. The answer of the past was for the trade routes to be tarmaced; the latest news from the present is of wilderness paths so badly damaged that, in their turn, they too have been tarmaced! And that is in the Australian outback of all places! Perhaps our children will yet be walking the Pennine Tarmac Way, helped not by Wainwright, but by strict lane controls. On balance, despite all my moans, I think I prefer to wallow through primeval swamp.

If, however, I had been interviewed halfway through the afternoon of Day Twenty, I would willingly have signed a petition in favour of a six-lane motorway to run the full

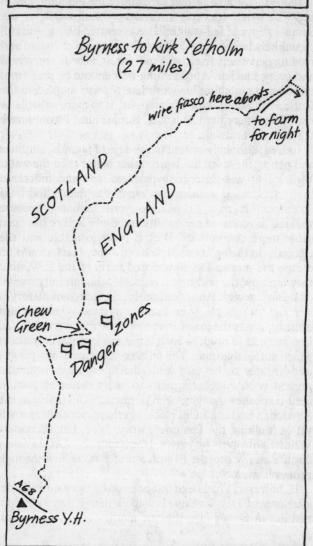

MAP 9: SECT. A

Byrness to kirk Yetholm
(27 miles)

wire fiasco here abouts

to farm
for night

SCOTLAND

ENGLAND

chew
Green

zones

Danger

A68

Byrness Y.H.

length of the Pennines, and the Cheviots. I never came closer to disaster than that afternoon. The path obligingly follows a wire fence along the Border for miles; so does a bog. To avoid a particular section which had the tell-tale vomit-green colour that indicates a depth of water in excess of the Mindanao Deep, I decided to bypass it by climbing along the wire. (If charged with the offence of damage to property, I shall blame the above sentence on a distracted printer.) There were two strands of wire some two feet apart; unfortunately, they had been made of an unusual compound: wire elastic. As I set foot on the bottom strand, it gave way about eighteen inches. I then grabbed the top strand to steady myself, which in turn gave way about three feet. The distance between hands and feet was thus over six foot – which I am not. As the weight of the upper half of my body pulled the top strand toward me, the force of the lower part of my body pushed the bottom strand away from me, and before I could so much as say, 'Oh blast!' I found myself with my legs and arms at full stretch and my body running parallel to the ground (or, to be exact, water). I was also facing upwards, so that if I fell it would be into a situation requiring instant command of the backstroke. Unfortunately, any form of backstroke seemed unlikely as I was firmly strapped to the sort of weight normally attached, according to The News of The World, to unwanted torsos. As I hung there I tried to remember what I could of Douglas Fairbanks senior's more agile films; however, the only comfort I could draw from them was that at least I was not being simultaneously attacked by pirates. I tried to lie still – if not actually to enjoy it – and then, in a series of controlled lurches, I managed to slide first my arms, and next my legs, over the wires, and painstakingly worked my way back toward the fence-post whence I came. And finally I executed the little-performed double-spinning sideways Fosbury loop jump. With one bound, I was . . . well, not so much free, as face down in the mud. It was after this I gradually began to tire of the Cheviots.

Matters then got rapidly worse. Sometimes a walk feels

never-ending, but the day's visibility was so marvellous that I could see it *was* never-ending. In fact, all that was ending was the day. To my horror, I calculated that I had walked 50 per cent of the final section and taken 95 per cent of the time available, thus incurring penalty points. I was faced with a choice of sleeping arrangements: I could either re-structure a large cairn, as a tombstone, or make for the one and only farmhouse that I could find on the map – a long, long hour's detour. It was the faintest and steepest of paths through wet and matted long grass, and I tripped and fell and rolled as much as I walked. It was almost dark when I arrived, soaked and bruised and muddy, and if I had been a pub landlord I would have had myself thrown off the premises.

The farm was extraordinarily remote, remote with several capital Rs. When the winter winds make moan there, only the helicopter calls. The services provided by the authorities were so few that it was a wonder the council didn't pay the owner rates. A bath, my first request, came with water freshly bubbled from the river – and, therefore, on reflection, from aforementioned vomit-green bogs? – but it was presumably up to minimum hygiene standards since, behind the taps, there appeared to be several Water Board officials gargling it thoroughly first. The taps, incidentally, were part of an ancient bath whose dimensions were so large that I could have registered several Olympic qualifying times. But I was not in the mood, and my second request was for a meal, which perhaps predictably, proved of equally generous size. And then, after dinner, the farmer, who was pushing 70, but pushing it with more muscle than most of us have at 40, sat back and waxed if not lyrical at least voluminous. And until gone midnight a lifetime's collection of Cheviot tales poured forth. Of which the most remarkable was the tale of the telephones.

For many years he had wanted a telephone. And for many years the GPO had quoted him a price only marginally cheaper than launching his own telecommunications satellite. A stalemate lasted for over a decade, until one day he was made an offer so remarkably cheap as to suggest the GPO had become a registered charity. Baffled, bewildered, but not bothered, he accepted. The phone was duly installed with ×miles of cable, and all went well until the annual snowdrifts fell and then the line went dead.

'Ah!' said the Polar engineer who had struggled through. 'Your fault's somewhere under 600 tons of snow.'

'So that's it till next spring, then?' said the farmer.

'Oh no! We'll give you one of the other lines.'

'Other lines? What other lines?' asked the farmer.

'Well, you've got seventeen running through here,' said the engineer.

'Seventeen!' said the farmer. And that was how he learnt about the proposed nuclear waste tip behind his farm . . . Just above the source of his river. . . . In an area known for earth tremors.

This is not a cautionary tale; it is almost a typical one. For much of its route the Pennine Way is less a wilderness walk than a tour of the damage done to wilderness; even in this remote fastness the Forestry Commission is now starting to gouge its tracks and trenches up across the hillsides. Like a rich man trying to get to heaven through a needle, the path has to thread its way to Scotland through everything from poison gas signs to water works, from abandoned army camps to rusting weather masts. The Ministry of Defence, in particular, seems to regard semi-dereliction as the natural state of buildings; presumably structures still intact are a sign of failure to the military mind. But every conceivable Government body from the Water Board to the Forestry Commission is at work, ensuring, as Wainwright puts it, that 'all kinds of fancy contraptions in wire enclosures desecrate the skyline.' If there were a single Government department officially called 'Destruction of the Environment' it could not be more effective – although some argue that it already exists and is called the Ministry of Agriculture.

Even that last bastion of freedom – silence – has seemingly gone for ever. Now one is alone with the larks, the curlews, and the nuclear bombers. And the nuclear bombers fly lowest of all. There is no escape any more – even if you go to the ends of the world, the end of the world comes with you. As I climbed up and away that last day, and the first jet of the morning loosened my bowels, I decided that next time out I would forget the waterproofs and the packed lunch, and just take a rucksack-sized, heat-seeking Sam missile. Given the consensus view of walkers, it should soon be standard YHA equipment.

It was hard to summon up the enthusiasm of D-Day for D-Day Two. The thought of yesterday's companions safely on a warm train home depressed me. So did the weather. As the path rose, still clinging to the border, to over 2,400 ft, so the mist fell, once again. And then the peat-hags returned, with virulence, once again. And still the miles ground on. An overpoweringly weary sense of *déjà vu*, *déjà marché*, *déjà souffert*, *déjà everything* bore in on me. I heard voices advising me to give up and wait for a vacant St Bernard to pass by. At one point, in a mixture of exhaustion and frustration, I even attempted the direct trans-bog approach, a technique from the call-my-bluff school of walking; the Romans may have been able to walk in a straight line for ever and a *dies*, but my efforts ended in instant decline and fall. All in all, as I edged onwards, there was just one small satisfaction to be had: to meet people with 250 miles still to go – and to tell them the worst was yet to come.

Surprisingly, the quickest 2½ miles of the whole Pennine Way occurred on this last section. At Cairn Hill, the path takes a detour to the summit of the Cheviot and back, a climb up to 2,676 feet through indescribable black ooze and impenetrable grey mist. I obtained a record time by not going. My mental state was beyond ethics.

Equally, my bodily state was now beyond physic, so, a mile further on, when I came across an abandoned railway truck, map ref. 877202, I called in for a brief collapse. How this truck arrived 1,800 feet up a bare mountain next to Scotland is a transport mystery second only to Stonehenge;

MAP 9: SECT·B

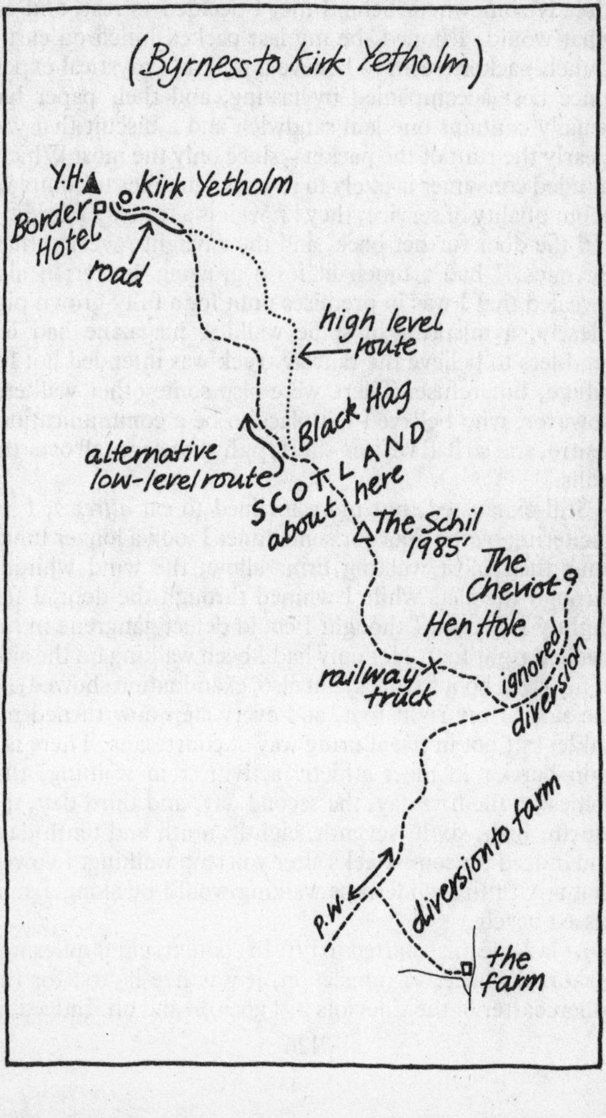

(Byrness to Kirk Yetholm)

Y.H.
Border Hotel
Kirk Yetholm
road

high level route

Black Hag

alternative low-level route

SCOTLAND about here

The Schil 1985'

The Cheviot

Hen Hole

railway truck

ignored diversion

P.W.

diversion to farm

the farm

without any tracks even the pre-Beeching railway service must have been somewhat limited here.

There were now just eight miles to go. With eight miles already somewhere behind me, I decided to rest, and eat what would, I hoped, be my last packed lunch on earth. Lunch-packers seem to believe a walk is a mystical experience best accompanied by fasting, and their paper bag usually contains one jam sandwich and a biscuit that was clearly the runt of the packet – since only the most Which-minded consumer is likely to re-walk ten miles to complain about quality of service, they know it is a feeder's market. I slid the door further back, and the daylight revealed that, for once, I had a lunch fit for a growing walker; it also revealed that I was in premises unfit for a fully-grown pig. Clearly, a misprint in some walking magazine had led ramblers to believe the railway truck was intended not for refuge, but refuse. There were also some other walkers, however, who believed the place to be a communications centre, and so had written short, pithy messages all over the walls.

Still exhausted, but more inclined to eat *alfresco*, I sat sheltering by the door for some time. I took a longer lunch hour than most walking firms allow, the wind whining through the slats while I whined through the door. I felt slightly sick, and I thought I could detect gangrene in my swollen right foot. Not only had I been walking on the side of my right boot for days, but also, examination showed, on the side of my right foot, and every step now turned my ankle, but not in the alluring way of courtesans. There is a pain barrier in most athletic activities; in walking, this comes on the first day, the second day, and third day, the fourth, fifth, sixth, seventh, eighth, ninth and tenth day, and indeed for some weeks after you stop walking. I vowed that any future wilderness walking would be along a sun-kissed beach.

At last the mist started to lift. In context, eight miles was a short distance; in translation, it was five hours, for the rollercoaster of the Cheviots just goes on and on. Indeed, it

was all the fun of the fair hereabouts. Wainwright strongly recommends a visit to a nearby ravine, Hen Hole, to search for rare wild flowers, and then later on he suggests a little light rock-climbing at the summit of The Schil, 1,985 ft high. They were temptations fairly easily resisted. But I had got to within four miles of home when I was more successfully seduced at Black Hag. Here the final choice has to be made: the high-level route or low-level route, for good weather or bad. I succumbed. On the strength of a distant white-flecked cloud I took the low road. And road was what it painfully became. The last two miles were agony, the final lap not even having the decency to be flat.

Nevertheless, when all is said and done, despite all the moans and groans, one impressive fact is undeniable – the walk is the most gruelling test of endurance imaginable, only completed by the finest, fittest specimens of true manhood . . . or, at least, so I thought, until on the last half-mile I was overtaken by two 8-year-olds who, with puffing parents in tow, actually sprinted over the finishing line (from the high-level route). Slightly discomfited, I made my way into the Border Hotel, the pub at journey's end, only to be bought a drink by a 65-year-old, just ahead of me, who said he had waited till retirement to do the walk. (I asked what he usually did for a holiday, and he said the previous year he and his wife had driven their Ford Anglia across the Gobi Desert.) I then turned, more modestly, to sign the Book of Honour kept in the pub – and saw the two previous signatories were aged 72 and 74, and, underneath 'Comments', had written 'A Good Pub Crawl'. Under the space for 'Time Taken' I had just written 21 days, when another finisher walked through the door, signed the book, and next to his name wrote '9 days'.

'How?' I asked incredulously.

'I cycled,' he said.

'All the way?' I asked even more incredulously.

'Oh no!' he said dismissively. 'Just downhill. I carried it the rest of the way.'

And then everyone, children and all, sat down for a good

meal of something and chips, to be followed, no doubt, by a great evening of stories. I thought the depths of human achievement had been exhaustively plumbed – but then a punk came in. He too had just finished.

'Did you enjoy it?' I asked.

'Great!' he said. 'I'm going to start straight back tomorrow!'

GLOSSARY OF DIFFICULT TECHNICAL TERMS

Anorak	a waterproof that lets in rain
Ascent	the most difficult type of walking apart from descent
Blister	highly recommended excuse for giving up walking
Bog	receptacle for keeping disused walkers in
Boot	device for obtaining blister
Bootlace	a long piece of cord which will convert effortlessly to short pieces of cord
Car	sexual fantasy of walkers

Cloud	mist in search of a walker
Compass	instrument for establishing you are lost
Countryside	the longest way between two towns
Cow	bull in sheep's clothing
Cripple	successful Pennine Way walker
Downhill	see uphill
Desert	area occasionally visited by lost Pennine Way walkers
Equipment	the 500 items essential for a walk
Exhaustion	the result of lifting the equipment
Fauna	rarely-seen Latin animals
Flora	margarine
Forest	form of cash used by Forestry Commission
Hill	a mountain by any other name
Hostel	accommodation providing a short, sharp shock
Hypothermia	illness suffered in hostels
Kinder Scout	error of nature
Lake	a high-level path after rain
Landscape	old-fashioned term, used to describe countryside before the existence of Water Authorities and Forestry Commission
Limp	distinguishing feature of walker
Mist	trainee fog, always found near walkers
MoD	organisation responsible for spoiling a good walk with death
Moorland	less land, more water
Mountain	a view obscured by mist
Mud	a substance causing one to be thrown out of pubs
Nature	see nurture (obs. Shak. joke)
Overland	method of travel much inferior to the underground
Pennine Way	undefined
Quagmire	good quality path
Quicksand	quite good quality path

Rain	good Pennine Way weather
Reservoir	large container of rain
Rucksack	small container of rain
Se promener avec	to do the Pennine Way with a foreigner
Signpost	rare piece of wood with faded illegible writing
Sing song	form of jollity favoured by adult walkers with mental age of five
Stile	method of separating fat walkers from thin walkers
Tent	device for channelling water through sleeping bag
Thermos	indispensable piece of equipment usually left at home
Torch	method of signalling you are lost to other people who are lost
Tree	receptacle for acid rain
Uphill	see downhill

Valley	the soggy bit between two hills
View	position from where sight of the soggy bits is obscured by mist
Warden	National Parks official responsible for preventing nature from escaping
Waterbottle	courage in the face of rain
Watershed	flooded greenhouse
Weather	(never permitting)
Whistle	for use, when injured, to attract wolves
Xercise	a way to die outdoors instead of in
Youth	the age at which old men start the Pennine Way

BIBLIOGRAPHY

Bradshaw's Railway Timetable
YHA Handbook
St John's Ambulance First Aid Manual

ANY FOOL CAN BE A PIG FARMER
by James Robertson

A walloping, rollicking, trotter's eye view of life as a pig farmer in North Wales.

Cats, dung, and overdrafts are the three things you can be sure of finding on every farm. But on James Robertson's farm there were also rats, bats, and a boa constrictor. And of course there were the pigs . . .

Sow Number Seven, Queen of the Pen and winner of all the porcine gang wars.

George, who was supposed to father piglets on all the tribe, but fell in love with Number Eleven and wore all the hair from her back.

Duke, whose idea of being sexy was to come galumphing up and take a jump at the sow of his choice. As he weighed the best part of a ton several promising romances were squashed until he was put on a diet.

James Robertson was kicked, bitten, piddled on, and infected with pig lice. But he survives and lives to tell the tale in *Any Fool Can Be A Pig Farmer*.

0 552 12399 4   £1.75

ANY FOOL CAN BE A COUNTRYMAN
by James Robertson

After pig farming there was dairy farming, and after dairy farming James Robertson thought he'd try his hand at running a bed and breakfast house in an old mill, and sometimes inside the mill too. There was also Bill, who padded round the garden at night with a shotgun, looking for Hitler. There were shoots where the visitors fell into slurry pits and the pheasants sat and watched. There were hunts where a corpse followed the hounds in a Land Rover. There were irrate farmers, village rows, ramblers, drunks, warlocks and cricket matches.

And at the end of it all James Robertson decided that people were just as peculiar as pigs and cows, and that he had at last become a full blown countryman.

0 552 12560 1   £1.75

HOVEL IN THE HILLS
by Elizabeth West

A warm, funny, moving account of the simple life in rural Wales.

She was a typist. He was a mechanic. One day Elizabeth and Alan West did what many people spend a lifetime dreaming of doing – they took to the hills. *Hovel in the Hills* is the story of the first nine years of their new life in a semi-derelict farmhouse overlooking Snowdonia. It is a heart-warming and salutary tale that abounds with the joys, and the dilemmas, of opting out of the rat race.

'Mrs West writes in a lively, humorous, down-to-earth style . . . an absorbing account of a brave experiment' *Sunday Times*

'I don't think I have read a better book of its kind . . . Mrs West writes remarkably well with just the right element of humour' *Daily Telegraph*

'The best book I have read about getting away from it all' *Western Mail*

'Conveys the joy in the countryside, in wild things and in coping for oneself' *The Times*

0 552 10907 X   £1.50

SUFFER LITTLE CHILDREN
by Elizabeth West

School secretaries are always middle-aged and wear old jumpers and tweed skirts that don't show the dirt. They sit surrounded by elastoplasts, wet knickers in plastic bags ('Angela has done it again. Have you a spare pair in your cupboard?'), confiscated lead-weighted coshes and obscene magazines, and tins of dinner money. They cope with threatening parents, infant sadists, leaking toilets, head lice, and the Education Authority.

At St. Claude's there was also the staff (mixed adults) and the children (mixed infants) who included Marlene, an enchanting five year old sex maniac, and the Hulberts, a three generational clan of affectionate criminals.

School secretaries are capable, cheerful, enterprising, resourceful, and also – after the first five years – very very mad.

0 552 12513 X   £1.75

THE BOOK OF NARROW ESCAPES
by Peter Mason
Illustrated by McLachlan

'So there I was, hurtling hysterically earthwards at 185 miles an hour, head down, with a useless rip-cord tightly clenched in my white-knuckled fist, with roughly ten seconds to live . . .'

It may – or may not – have been at this point that author Peter Mason came up with the bestselling idea of *The Book of Narrow Escapes*. What is certain is that he has gathered together some of the most hilarious, mind-boggling and spine-chilling brushes with death, the law and all sorts of other forces outside our normal control for this brilliantly illustrated volume.

The Book of Narrow Escapes is a highly amusing, and occasionally terrifying collection of what might have been if the gods of luck had been looking the other way.

0 552 12436 2 . £1.50

A SELECTED LIST OF HUMOUR TITLES
AVAILABLE FROM CORGI BOOKS

WHILE EVERY EFFORT IS MADE TO KEEP PRICES LOW, IT IS SOME-
TIMES NECESSARY TO INCREASE PRICES AT SHORT NOTICE. CORGI
BOOKS RESERVE THE RIGHT TO SHOW NEW RETAIL PRICES ON
COVERS WHICH MAY DIFFER FROM THOSE PREVIOUSLY ADVERTISED
IN THE TEXT OR ELSEWHERE.

THE PRICES SHOWN BELOW WERE CORRECT AT THE TIME OF GOING
TO PRESS (MAY '86).

All these books are available at your book shop or newsagent, or can be ordered direct from the publisher. Just tick the titles you want and fill in the form below.

CORGI BOOKS, Cash Sales Department, P.O. Box 11, Falmouth, Cornwall.

Please send cheque or postal order, no currency.

Please allow cost of book(s) plus the following for postage and packing:

U.K. Customers—Allow 55p for the first book, 22p for the second book and 14p for each additional book ordered, to a maximum charge of £1.75.

B.F.P.O. and Eire—Allow 55p for the first book, 22p for the second book plus 14p per copy for the next seven books, thereafter 8p per book.

Overseas Customers—Allow £1.00 for the first book and 25p per copy for each additional book.

NAME (Block Letters) ....

ADDRESS ....

....